The Sociology of Sacred Texts

The
Sociology
of
Sacred Texts

Edited by
Jon Davies & Isabel Wollaston

Sheffield Academic Press

Copyright © 1993 Sheffield Academic Press

Published by Sheffield Academic Press Ltd
343 Fulwood Road
Sheffield S10 3BP
England

Typeset by Sheffield Academic Press
and
Printed on acid-free paper in Great Britain
by Bookcraft (Bath) Limited
Bath

British Library Cataloguing in Publication Data

Sociology of Sacred Texts
    I. Davies, Jon II. Wollaston, Isabel
    306.6

ISBN 1-85075-404-7

Contents

Contents

7

Acknowledgments

This book contains a selection of the papers delivered at a conference, 'The Sociology of Sacred Texts', held at the University of Newcastle upon Tyne, 1–4 July 1991. Some of the papers have been revised for publication, others are in their original form. In order to retain the original character of the papers and facilitate publication, we have kept corrections and alterations to a minimum.

We would like to thank all those who attended, or expressed interest in attending, the conference. In particular, we would like to thank Professor John Sawyer of the Department of Religious Studies, University of Newcastle upon Tyne, who had the original idea of holding such a conference and who was responsible for much of the organization. We would also like to thank Mrs Gloria Andreasen for her help in preparing the typescript of this volume; and Michael Burke, Carol Charlton and Charlotte Porter for assisting with the organization of the conference. Finally, we are grateful to Helen Tookey of Sheffield Academic Press and Paul Joyce of the Department of Theology, University of Birmingham, for their helpful editorial comments.

List of Abbreviations

CBQMS	*Catholic Biblical Quarterly*, Monograph Series
HUCA	*Hebrew Union College Annual*
OBO	Orbus biblicus et orientalis
PMLA	*Publications of the Modern Language Association*
SPB	Studia postbiblica
WUNT	Wissenschaftliche Untersuchungen zum Neuen Testament

List of Contributors

Linda Anderson lectures in English at the University of Newcastle upon Tyne.

Patrizia Burdi teaches at the department of Glotto-Anthropological Studies at La Sapienza University, Rome, Italy.

Mark Chapman lectures in systematic theology at Ripon College, Cuddesdon, Oxford.

Jon Davies is a sociologist and Head of the Department of Religious Studies at the University of Newcastle upon Tyne.

Rosalind I.J. Hackett teaches at the University of Tennessee, Knoxville, USA.

Irén Lovász teaches at the JP University, Pécs, Hungary.

Alessandro Lupo teaches at the Department of Glotto-Anthropological Studies at La Sapienza University, Rome, Italy.

Michael Mach teaches in the Department of Jewish Philosophy in the University of Tel Aviv, Israel.

Jacob Neusner is Distinguished Research Professor of Religious Studies at the University of South Florida, USA.

Lauren Pfister teaches at the Hong Kong Baptist College.

Kathleen Thomas was until recently an MLitt student in the Department of Religious Studies, University of Newcastle upon Tyne.

Jonathan Webber is the Frank Green Fellow in Jewish Social Studies at the Oxford Centre for Postgraduate Hebrew Studies.

Isabel Wollaston is Lecturer in Theology, University of Birmingham.

Introduction

Jon Davies and Isabel Wollaston

Words of God are not like any other text: but they have to be constructed—printed, edited, proof-read, authorized, reviewed—like any other text. They are, that is to say, both timeless and transient, transcendental and mundane, declared and debated, universal and particular, ancient and contemporary, dead and alive. Human beings have sought to understand sacred texts in various ways.

Theologians examine sacred texts to establish, in an authentic (usually the earliest) version of the text, the truth about God: they try to answer the *'what* is the text?' question. In the conference of which this volume is the result, Jacob Neusner stated that he was interested only in documents which were collective, anonymous, authoritative, proclaimed; and while the paper he gave did acknowledge that texts arise in social contexts, he was essentially working within that scholarly tradition which takes the given text as the basic datum and object of analysis.

Social scientists—archaeologists, anthropologists, sociologists—are more inclined to ask the *'who* is the text?' question. They wish to know what are the social relations of production which (in a variety of notions of causality) lie behind, or give rise to, or have an 'elective affinity' with, a particular text and its transformations—or lack of transformations, since the absence of change can, just as easily as its presence, require theories of social causation. Who wrote the text, and with whom?

The use of the term 'elective affinity' will alert readers to the presence of Max Weber (and all the problems he causes!). Weber was concerned with the 'who' question; his aim was to analyse the role of religion in the world. The study of religion in the world was and is a very different task from that of studying the world's religions; and again we are back to the major difference between theologians and social scientists.

In *The Protestant Ethic and the Spirit of Capitalism*, Weber claimed to find in Calvinism a doctrine (Predestination) which, he argued, became associated ('elective affinity') with the dominant force of rational capitalism; that is to say he was explicitly interested in the role of religion as an ally of the hegemonic ideology in the process of the economic transformation of Europe—and the world. In a way, this focus on ruling ideas and ruling classes complements such social commentary as theologians might occasionally produce, because their own interest in *canonical* texts leads, explicitly or not, to a focus on the doings of the authoritative or dominant ecclesiastical class. A mirror image of this focus is an interest in oppressed or revolutionary socio-religious movements, where hegemony and hegemonic religions are under explicit refutational and political attack. The opposition of these two extremes has high dramatic visibility and fairly extensive historical documentation. The doings of 'ordinary people', the middling sort of folk, are very much more opaque: and in as much as most of the 'middling folk' of the world are brown, or black, or women, or children, there are huge gaps in both the sociological and theological archive.

In the ethnographies of anthropology is to be found a specific type of social science; that is, descriptions of 'whole-culture' systems, presented as being rooted in a more or less homogeneous value system (often an explicitly religious value system), a system empirically available to the observant and inquisitive anthropologist in drama, ritual, and public praying and dance. Our conference, serendipitously perhaps, heard many papers which implicitly and explicitly sought to apply this basic model to more heterogeneous or divided cultures: the idea of the 'vernacular', for example, can be derived from the basic anthropological ideas on 'patterns of culture', although it must be used with care when dealing, as we were, with pluralistic societies in which religious texts can be both ideological *and* vernacular or populist in character. It is also, of course, much more difficult for an observer of contemporary society and its religious practices to be as genuinely ubiquitous a participant observer as the anthropologist can be. Having said this, it will be clear from the contents of this book that there is more of Durkheim in it than of Max Weber (although he is unavoidable in these kinds of discussion!); and that many contributors owe much to writers such as Bronislaw Malinowski, George Tyrell, Arnold van Gennep, Mircea Eliade, Ernst Troeltsch, Victor Turner, Jacob Neusner and Peter Berger.

In selecting papers for the book, we paid particular attention to those papers which described sacred texts *in the making*, as enacted ritual dramas or myth-making, where ordinary people, operating perhaps within a broader culture, construct their own versions of the sacred in order to be able to live with and make some kind of sense of the troubled worlds they live in: war, death, illness, slavery, slaughter. In this century these are the experience of us all; they are ordinary experiences, no longer the odd accident in an otherwise stable life, but the ceaselessly returning dramas of a world turned upside down by the force of Western expansion set in train by Columbus, the Genoese male Pandora. Whether in the wars and bigotries of Old Europe, or the genocides of Latin America, or the slaveries of Africa and the Atlantic, men and women find themselves living in a history which has more ghouls and ghosts within it than were imagined in even the direst of earlier demonologies, theologies and liturgies. The simple truth about the sacralizations of the past is that they no longer suffice, either as words or as authority, as litany or as liturgy. In Europe, and the other worlds over which Europe has spread, Christianity, after two thousand years of mission, has indeed become the basic underlying archaeology of belief, the vernacular mythology, a necessary but not sufficient part of our religious quest. Jon Davies' paper argues that death in war cannot be dealt with by the laconic formulations of traditional funerary liturgies; and the papers by Isabel Wollaston and Jonathan Webber describe the struggles over the meaning of the past implicit in the attempt by Jews and Christians to unwrap the gift of Auschwitz–Birkenau, the capital of Europe. Patrizia Burdi, Irén Lovász and Alessandro Lupo, in three separate papers, present an account of praying—praying, that is, as an enactment, an act of selectivity, of creative practical liturgy-making, as peasants in Mexico and southeastern Europe adapt for their own purposes both the Christianity they have been taught and the much older paganisms they remember.

Mark Chapman and Lauren Pfister both address the Max Weber problematic—but do so again in the context of a society which Weber predicted rather than described. America may well have avoided Europe's wars, but capitalism bounded forward in America in ways which the multifarious little feudalisms of Weber's Germany would not have permitted; and free of these trammels, capitalist Chicago grew at a rate and in ways productive of a rather disturbing set of social problems. In Chicago, the staff of the new university, in both the Divinity School and the Sociology Faculty, sought to derive, from (on the one hand) the teachings of Jesus of Nazareth and (on the other) the lessons of American positivism, an antidote to the unintended consequences of American capitalism's success: the crime, poverty and violence of the exploding city, and the lack of an ethic of communal sense of responsibility on the part of a business elite whose very success proved (to themselves at least) the prime value of unrestricted individualism. On the other side of the world, in a China which had also been set the Weberian catechism, another society faced the corrosive force of both capitalism and imperialism with a traditional religious system which seemed, from the Weberian analysis, doomed to fail. Pfister dissects both analysis and system, showing (again!) that Weber rather over-simplified things; but rather more interestingly perhaps he shows how the pressure on Western culture to 'understand' China so affected the task of the main translator of the Confucian canon (James Legge) that it was, in effect, mispresented to scholars such as Weber!

Kathleen Thomas's paper on the Quaker *Book of Discipline* puts us onto a very different scale from that of the Chinese Empire. Quakers (the Religious Society of Friends) are few in number, perhaps 200,000 in the world. As a sect derived from the English Civil War period, they have a 'canon' (they themselves would be loth to call it a sacred text) founded in the era of the printing press; and as an unusually methodical people they have texts which have been and are changed to the accompaniment of carefully stated reasons: little needs to be tendentiously inferred from, or imputed to, the text-changers of the Religious Society of Friends. Thomas charts the steady alteration in substance and style of a religious movement gradually abandoning the stance of being 'in the world but not of it'. Sacred texts, as insisted-upon truths, are the boundary markers of religious groups, the available 'test' of membership. This paper raises two interesting questions: is it, contrary to common sense, perhaps easier to change a written text than to change an oral tradition; and do sacred texts which are changed in order to make accommodation with the world thereby lose their religious as well as social function?

The book's fourth section is a selection from a number of contributions which in tone and total show how much that passes for 'academic' discussion of the sociology of sacred texts is in fact too often a discussion of 'official' texts by semi-official men, most often men from the better-off parts of the world. We, as editors, are painfully aware that our conference, excellent and good fun though it was, was clearly limited by the inherited built-in privileges of gender, place, language and money (of which more later); and our eventual selection for publication, even though fairly balanced on the gender issue, must surely fail the test of 'representativeness' when that test is applied, as it should be, on a global scale.

The contributions of Rosalind Hackett and Linda Anderson are then to be doubly welcomed, because they try to deal with a section of humanity which is almost totally absent in the texts of the world, and in sacred texts and canonical texts in particular: women. Hackett discusses the growing competence of women's Pentecostal/evangelical groups in Nigeria, and Anderson discusses Toni Morrison's novel *Beloved*. In both content and, in the case of the novel, style, these discussions of women's relationship to the content and style of traditional sacred texts requires a rethinking of the whole function and social location of text-creating and text-sacralizing. Africa south of the Sahara is a predominantly Christian continent; but it is an area still (and permanently?) only marginally involved in the world economy: it produces only 1 per cent of the world's wealth (that is, it is essentially redundant); it is experiencing rapid population growth, and a fair amount of trouble from economic debt, civil war and a speedily advancing AIDS epidemic. It is hard to believe that women will not be called upon to take the brunt of this—indeed, they already have; and Hackett shows how a feminist (but not in the Western sense of that word) approach to biblical interpretation and religious practice is beginning to lay a theological basis for a distinctively female religiosity. Anderson makes one very clear point: while the sacred can perhaps be found in a black woman's agonized attempt to see herself in her history, this attempt, as a sacred text, must be actively and quietly listened to *as it forms*, rather than demanded as finished canon, because the history is too painful to be so expressed or so commanded. Do sacred texts, in the conventions of male history, only become canonical when they lose subjective reality or fecundity—and therefore become amenable to grammar?

The book concludes with two papers by Michael Mach and Jacob Neusner which offer more traditional interpretations of the symbiotic relationship between sacred texts and their environment.

The last point we want to make in this Introduction is one already alluded to—indeed, one referred to immediately above. There is a world hegemonic system, with an active, interventionist, influential and powerful core, an ignored and passive periphery, and various bits in between. This is not simply a geographical system, though it is mappable; it has built into it the cross-cutting variables of gender, class, race and age. Most sacred texts are the products of what some radical Americans call DWEMS (Dead White European Males); look at a picture of the Council of Trent. There is absolutely no need to go so far as some radical Americans, and dismiss the entire product of the DWEMS as mere self-serving propaganda; but even on such a small scale as our conference it was clear that money, boundary problems, family commitments, language, political regimes and so on were all major determinants of who could come and therefore of what was said. The conference, that is, was a little paradigm of the 'Sociology of Sacred Texts'. We had expressions of interest from men in China, India and Africa, backed by requests for financial help we were unable to provide; and no doubt in those, and other, parts of the world there were and are lots of good and holy women who did not bother to reply, even though they would have loved to come, because they were immobilized by the endless things that immobilize women.

How different would Nicea have been if all the people who were invited had been able to go? Or if those who were unable to actually go could have sent their views in over the fax? Or if the whole thing had been televised? Or written in Kiswahili or Hausa? Or run by women?

It must surely be the case that a compilation of all the existing sacred texts of the world, together with a photographic album of their authors, would give us the writings and a picture of a lot of rather well-to-do elderly white or light brown men.

Most of the world has been forgotten by history; and this, given the propensity of men to canonize themselves, must be truer of sacred texts than of most other texts. This is in large measure why we have tried, in this book, to maintain a fairly wide definition of 'sacred text' and to promote the discussion of the process of sacralization as something other than mere argument about the variety of editions of a book or the etymologies of a word. Human beings are endlessly resacralizing the world and their place in it; the rate of social change is now so great, and of such discontinuity, that the great churches of the last thousand years may well end up as sects, and their great canons as mysteries of, by, and for, the few; but men and women will continue to find in the inevitabilities of their lives with each other endless occasion to pray and to re-enact the sacred in ways which will draw on but not be limited to traditions and memories of traditions. We hope that this book, in a very small way, will be part of this process of reactivation of the tradition of the sacred—as an activity reaching out into and opening up our increasingly-one world, rather than as something closing off and anxiously protecting bits of an ancient canon as something too precariously precious to be offered up.

Part 1: Memorials

Introduction to Part 1: Memorials

Jon Davies and Isabel Wollaston

Memories are an essential part of human existence, helping us to shape and define our sense of who we are, where we come from and how we should relate to those around us. In short, without memory we would have no identity. Memorials are the lapidary texts of memory, expressing what and whom a community considers it important to remember. To paraphrase Jon Davies, the impulse to build memorials arises, in part, from the refusal of the living (or, more specifically, those who survived) to let the dead die.

Recent work in this area suggests that there are two basic approaches to understanding memorials. The first insists that memorials should be capable of standing on their own, that they should be self-explanatory, containing sufficient information concerning the events and individuals being commemorated to anchor them in the public's consciousness. From this perspective, the function of memorials is to provide an accurate, unbiased record of the period of history being remembered. By contrast, the second approach (reflected in the three papers in this section) argues that memorials are representations or reconstructions of the past. As such, they are inevitably selective in what and whom they represent and how it is represented. To expect a memorial to be self-critical is to misunderstand its function: by their very nature, memorials mediate history. They therefore also inevitably contain the potential to *revise* history. The decision to build a memorial requires an act of deliberate choice, an act of both *inclusion* and *exclusion*: these lapidary texts clearly express who is (and implicitly, who is not) considered to be part of the history of a particular community (it goes without saying that there are relatively few memorials specifically commemorating the deeds of women). The controversies generated by memorials provide a microcosm of the wider struggle as to who will write history, and whose history will be written. The controversy generated by the inscription on the memorial at Auschwitz–Birkenau and the reconceiving of the Auschwitz site currently under way, described in Jonathan Webber's paper, is a case in point.

As well as serving as a reification of memory, memorials can also be interpreted as vernacular sacred texts, expressing the ways in which a particular community relates to major social or cultural issues. As such, they play an integral part in the process of myth-making. The three papers in this section illustrate the ways in which the World War (Jon Davies) and the Holocaust (Isabel Wollaston, Jonathan Webber) have been and are being mythologized.

The twentieth century has been indelibly scarred by the large-scale taking of life, through both war and state-sanctioned mass murder. The three papers in this section explore the emergence of 'vernacular' sacred texts in response to this phenomenon. Given that 'there is no social change greater than that brought about by war', it was inevitable that the experience of wars to end all wars would challenge, and even shatter, prevailing cultural, political, social and religious attitudes and beliefs. In his paper, Jon Davies suggests that the ubiquitous war memorials of Europe should be interpreted as sacred texts articulating a vernacular Christianity which rewrote 'official' theology and liturgy. If war memorials constitute a public response to the large-scale taking of life in war, then Holocaust memorials constitute a public response to state-sanctioned mass murder. These memorials are endeavouring to respond to the mass murder of approximately a third of world Jewry. In her paper Isabel Wollaston suggests that a vernacular Judaism has emerged, based on 'the myth of Holocaust and Redemption'. Jonathan Webber takes this suggestion a stage further and, drawing upon his own extensive fieldwork, argues that 'Jewish perceptions of the Holocaust today are so deeply contradictory that the very phenomenon has become mythologized'.

The controversy generated by memorials to either the Holocaust or to World War can often be traced to the contradictions inherent in Jewish perceptions of the event, or to conflict between these perceptions and those of other groups (such as the Poles in the case of Auschwitz). The passions aroused by such controversies (and there are parallels with war memorials, for example the annual disputes over the choice of appropriate hymns for Remembrance Sunday) only serve to illustrate the hold that such vernacular sacred texts continue to exercise over the communities from which they arise.

Lapidary Texts: A Liturgy Fit for Heroes?

Jon Davies

War memorials are a refusal by the living to let the dead die. As ritualized objects of remembrance, they represent a 'popular' or vernacular form of Christianity—*lex orandi, lex credendi*—centred on a restructured version of the Passion story's three themes of sacrificial death, betrayal and redemptive remembrance. As sacred texts, the war memorials of Europe, with their dead, mark out in iconography, epigraphy and geography the cultural and spatial boundaries of a 'Christian Europe' rooted in a particular concept of moral and military duty—as exemplified in the latest Gulf War.

A 'Sociology of Sacred Texts' clearly assumes that texts change, in style, in content, in scope, in line with social change; that there is, to use Max Weber's term, an 'elective affinity' between variations of text and variations of society. War is the most dramatic form of social change: the experience of battle the most dramatic change in a person's life.

The thesis of this paper is that the Great War of 1914–18 reordered Christian and in particular Protestant (Anglican) theology and liturgy. The direction of this reordering is best understood by reference to the ubiquitous war memorials of Europe (there are somewhere between 40,000 and 100,000 of these in the UK alone), the shrines, wayside liturgies and alfresco pulpits of the twentieth century. In iconography, epigraphy and geography these war memorials are the lapidary texts of a vernacular Christianity which rewrote 'establishment' theologies and liturgies on suffering, on war and on the death of young men in war.

Europe's war memorials indicate how Christianity became detached (or at least detachable) from jingoism/nationalism; and how, via a huge statement of the centrality of the crucified Christ (democratized in the armies of the dead), it came to find its clearest and most persuasive call to arms not in the shrill ambition of national victory but in the notion of dutiful sacrifice in the cause of universal values and virtues—the very purpose of the Passion of Christ.

The 1914–19 war memorial at Heriot's School, Edinburgh, carries the words 'Dulce et decorum est pro patria mori'. The 1939–45 memorial, immediately behind it, has on it the words 'They saw their duty plain, their lives they gave for Freedom, Truth and Right'.

60 million men were mobilized to fight in the Great War. While to historians war tends to be seen as some rather opaque thing which happens in between history, for these men war was what they did all day; 21 million of the 60 million were wounded and eight million were killed. The living were in no way minded to let their dead comrades die. The politics of war veterans in the 'twenty year truce' of the inter-war period varied considerably, from the quietism and pacifism of the French *Poilus* to the revanchism and semi-paganisms of the German *Stahlhelm*—with the British in between. World War Two, in which another 70 million Europeans were mobilized and in which another 15 million Europeans died, created another complexity of shared and diverse experiences; but the war memorial is a common theme, a liturgy in stone, a hymnody learned in battle: *lex orandi, lex credendi*.

Like most symbols, the war memorial is a symbol which divides as well as unites. In restating the meaning of war death, our war memorials, war cemeteries and their associated rituals reinvigorated and reinvigorate Christianity (for better or for worse!), and remobilize it for use on a broader European front. The boundaries of Christian Europe are, to paraphrase Kipling, 'marked out with our dead'.[1] War graves and war cemeteries, in Europe and overseas, identify both the abandoned far-flung ramparts of the Christian Empire as well as its fierce and fiercely theological heart.

1. R. Kipling, 'Take Up The White Man's Burden', in J. Cochrane (ed.), *The Penguin Rudyard Kipling* (Harmondsworth: Penguin, 1972): the verse refers to

> The Ports ye may not enter,
> The Roads ye may not tread:
> Go make them with your living,
> And mark them with your Dead!

War memorials are the most common form of public statuary. They are the ones most generally understood: 1914–1918 needs no explanation. They are religious and hallowed objects. They are regularly the centre of ritual activity. They are the remembered dead.

War memorials are neither unambiguously nor exclusively Christian artefacts. Whether in sculpture, inscription or location, they draw upon a wide range of religious and cultural meaning; classical and biblical words interact quite familiarly with secular, pagan and military sculpture, while the huge tragedy of self-sacrifice (as opposed to the taking of life) provides a very direct connection to the liturgical enactment of the story of Christ as Calvary. Clearly no European culture is coterminous with Christian religious symbols, and probably never was; but no European culture is either complete or comprehensible without them.

Pagan and Christian culture flow in and around the ritual activity which attends war memorials and war remembrance. In England, not an evening passes without somewhere, at a gathering of old 'Companions' (ex-servicemen), the young and beautiful dead being remembered with the words of Lawrence Binyon's poem 'For the Fallen':

> They went with songs to the battle, they were young,
> Straight of limb, true of eye, steady and aglow,
> They shall grow not old, as we that are left grow old:
> Age shall not weary them, nor the years condemn.
> At the going down of the sun and in the morning
> We shall remember them.[1]

Whether this is some modern version of the medieval doctrine of *contemptus mundi*, or whether it is part of a more general pre-Christian or universal idealization of young men killed in war, does not really matter. The young dead soldiers are, directly or indirectly, seen through the same light as the young dead Christ.

Remembrance thus becomes something other than a mere nationalistic or sectarian activity because the symbols and meanings of remembrance are so readily subsumed into Christianity, the common religion of Europe. The dead whose death is so comprehensibly

---

1. L. Binyon, 'For the Fallen', in J. Benn (ed.), *Memorials* (London: Ravette, 1986).

symbolized in the ubiquitous war memorials of Europe are a central part of the symbolic community which transcends the causes of conflict at the same time as it reinvokes them. The memorials (and the cemeteries) marking the deaths of the best we bred are the ways in which our culture is marked out by our dead. There is perhaps little need to point out how masculine this culture is.

Two methodological points. First, there is no 'catalogue' of European war memorials, although the Imperial War Museum is currently working on a 'National Inventory' for Britain; and there are partial surveys of memorials in France, Germany and Eastern Europe. References to war memorials must therefore be selective.

Secondly, the memorials cannot be fully understood except by reference to the range of social activities surrounding them—that is, their design and dedication, their annual reinvokings and their meaning to 'communities' of varying sizes and degrees of social cohesion. An analysis of these rituals is beyond the scope of this paper.

The major part of this investigation will try to locate the lapidary texts of the war memorial within the broader Christian liturgical tradition, while paying particular attention to the problems that war and war memorializing present to Protestant and Anglican attitudes to the dead. The simplest sociological point here is that there is no social change greater than war. The more complex sociological point is that when sacred texts, be they war memorials or holy documents, are viewed sociologically they cease to be comprehensible as theology and come to be seen as part of the broader symbolic constructs of a culture and of its history. In a secular world, theology is always subsumed into culture; and culture is a jumble sale.

The Reformation—regarded by some as a theological non-event as far as England was concerned—was to a large extent an attack upon the medieval church's theology, liturgy, administration and political economy of death. The general drift of the Reformers was to redefine death as an essentially private matter, undeserving of overmuch sacramental attention from the church—though few would perhaps go so far as the Puritan who advocated a ritual-free interment, followed by a sociable stomping down of the disturbed clods as the way of ritualizing the event.

Disputes about purgatory and predestination, offertories and chantries, martyrs and saints, icons and atonement and so on tended to leave Protestant Europe with a depleted liturgical and hagiographical competence in matters to do with death. In particular, the contempt for medieval martyrology tended to leave Christ as the main 'role model' when, in the twentieth century, millions of European Christians, Protestants and Catholics alike, had to face up to a violent death in war—a war for which there was no precedent and for which, very quickly, men were unable to see any sensible secular explanation or purpose. Calvary, the calvary of the Incognito Christ, was the only alternative to cynicism—or indeed, as I will argue, to pacifism. Calvary makes war liturgically respectable.

Distaste for the economic as well as the theological consequences of the doctrine of purgatory combined with the dogma of predestination and of substitutionary and penal atonement (of and by the Crucified, Hell-descended, Heaven-ascended Christ) to produce at least an indifferent or even disinterested funeral liturgy: 'Man that is born of woman hath but a short time to live. He cometh up and is cut down like a flower; he fleeth as it were a shadow, and never continueth in one stay' (Anglican funeral liturgy).

It may of course be objected that such liturgies were restricted in their disinterestedness to individual deaths only; yet the 'Official Notices' for examples of collective or mass death—in this case in coal mine disasters—indicates the strength of Protestant disinclination to register much more than the fact of the death of the dead (examples taken from documents in the possession of the Folk Museum of Wales, St Fagan's, Cardiff). In 1878, 264 men and boys died in an explosion at the Prince of Wales Pit, Abercarne. The official notice of the disaster carries Isa. 66.15-6: 'For, behold, the Lord will come with fire... and the slain of the Lord shall be many'. January 13, 1879, 63 men and boys, Dinas Colliery, Rhondda: 'Death comes in all shapes'. October 14, 1913, 434 colliers killed at Senghenydd Colliery: 'Boast not thyself of tomorrow: for thou knowest not what a day may bring forth'.

Clearly such theologies and liturgies could not simply sail serenely on in the face of even ordinary death-concerns, still less the huge irruption of bewilderment and grief caused by the Great War; but their dismissive strength is still writ large in the Protestant consciousness. Andrew Jones, in *Remembrance Sunday*, states that:

> The vocabulary of sacrifice is particularly problematic. The number of
> people who willingly laid down their lives as a sacrifice must have been

very few indeed. In simple terms, most fought to survive, not to die.
Many fought out of some sense of duty, and they too intended to survive.
It is better therefore to pray about those who were killed or who died,
rather than about those who laid down their lives or sacrificed
themselves.[1]

This is a fairly tactless bit of advice—the Rev. Jones's pamphlet is
meant to help clergy handle Remembrance Day congregations—
though even here the Christian inheritance enables the author to avoid
the theologically much more difficult problem of men who died while
actively trying to kill someone else, never mind those who came
heroically home having actually managed to kill *and* survive. Even
within the context of a Protestant theology of death in war the Rev.
Jones would find himself in serious trouble on Remembrance Day if
he were to insist on parading these views—not because much of what
he says is undoubtedly true, but because it denies what is probably the
major insistence of our war memorials' theology, that of the freely
given nature of the *sacrifice* made by the dead men they commemorate, and of the purpose for which they *gave* it:

> These gave their lives that you who live may reap
> A richer harvest ere you fall asleep (Shrewsbury War Memorial).

> When you go home,
> Tell them of us and say
> For your tomorrow
> We gave our today (Barnstable, Devon, and Kohima, Burma).

> Greater love hath no man than this
> That a man lay down his life for his friends (Jn 15.13).

The Rev. Jones's Protestant disinclination to view death in war as *eo
ipso* proof of 'good works' moves into a broader Christian controversy to which war memorials make a distinctive contribution, that is,
the question of sacrifice—of a man or men for a worldly cause, and of
the central sacrifice of Christianity, of Christ for all humankind, for
the sake of God, and as the only way of atonement. It is noteworthy
that Jones leaves out of his list of Remembrance hymns and songs the
1918 hymn 'O Valiant Hearts', with its reference to 'our lesser
calvaries', which gets as close to equating in hymnody the war dead
with Christ as do many of our war memorials in inscription and

---

1.   A. Jones, *Remembrance Sunday* (Nottingham: Grove Press, 1987), p. 20.

sculpture. In various ways, these war memorials claim for the war dead an association with that salvific potency which Christianity locates in the sacrifice of Christ; salvation for the dead because of the sacrificial nature of their (freely offered) death; and salvation for others, a substitutional atonement, for the same reason—and *as long as* they, the surviving others, remember.

The issue of salvation via good works versus salvation by grace alone is dealt with by being avoided: there is simply *no sin* in the pre-war or war-time soldier; *every* death is sacrifice; *all* the dead are saved; and collectively all of them have a salvific power for and of others—*as long as* they are properly remembered, not 'betrayed' by being forgotten.

The Incognito Christ

In Loving Memory and Sure Hope of Life Eternal
The King of the World shall raise us up
Who have died for his laws unto Everlasting Life (Hollybush, Worcs.).[1]

This Calvary was erected by their friends (Parish Church of St Augustine of Canterbury, Queen's Gate, Kensington).

They Died That We Might Live (Kilmartin, Argyllshire).

Be Thou Faithful Unto Death,
And I will Give You a Crown of Life (Great Milton, Oxon.).

True Love by Death is Tried (Saddleworth Moor, Oldham).

Through the Grave and Gate of Death we Pass
To Our Joyful Resurrection (St Leonard's Church, Sandridge, Herts.).

When you go Home
Tell them of us and say
For Your Tomorrow
We Gave Our Today (as above).

The Priest
Didst give thine only son Jesus Christ to suffer death upon the cross for our redemption: who made there (by His one oblation of himself once

---

1.   Individual war memorials are described in C. McIntyre, *Monuments of War* (London: Hale, 1990), and D. Boorman, *At the Going Down of the Sun* (York: The Ebor Press, 1988).

offered) a full perfect and sufficient sacrifice, oblation and satisfaction for the sins of the whole world . . . and did institute . . . a perpetual memory of that his precious death. . .

The People say
We offer and present unto thee, O Lord, ourselves, our souls and bodies, to be a reasonable, holy, and lively sacrifice unto thee. . . we beseech thee to accept this our bounden duty and service. . . (*Order of Holy Communion, The Book of Common Prayer*).

God so loved . . .
Greater love hath no man . . .

We have in war memorials, in their lapidary liturgies and in their associated social behaviour, a form of vernacular theology. In the past 'the vernacular' was synonymous with 'paganism', a force always threatening to irrupt into the anxiously missionizing, never secure, Christian Catholic church. Often this paganism derived from a more violent tradition and in its borrowings from Christianity would, for example, try to endow with martial competence various saints of the church whose canonization or standing in the church was for virtues other than those for which paganism was attempting to recruit them.

By the end of the nineteenth century the Europe which entered the Great War had had nearly two thousand years of Christian proselytization: *Christianity had become the vernacular*, while the church had perhaps become established and remote, and while the dominant thought systems had become or were becoming secular and indifferent to transcendental questions. The war, obviously, militarized nations; and states and governments anxiously sought and obtained (though often not as unreservedly as they hoped) national blessings for the national effort from the national church (that is, national church leaders). Yet the vernacular or popular culture did not respond with a re-militarized Christianity, but with a Eucharistic one, rooted in the idea of sacrifice and expressed in the language of duty. The nation's war memorials express this form of religion—and if the Parish Communion movement reflects anything it reflects this. But we have to be clear that this reinvigorated Catholicism did not produce a view of the war like that of the war poets; in and on our war memorials very few of our soldiers 'die as cattle' (Wilfred Owen, 'Anthem for Doomed Youth'[1]); and while national pride, regimental pride and

1. W. Owen, 'Anthem for Doomed Youth', in J. Silkin (ed.), *First World War*

village pride are all to be found on war memorials, the single most powerful statement is that of dutiful, voluntary, comradely self-sacrifice—the Eucharistic story. It is clearly significant that Remembrance Day celebrates not victory but the ceasefire. It is Remembrance Day, not a victory parade. Do this, in remembrance of me. . .

Why did war choose the Eucharist? War is a mixed experience; and it may well be that it was the particular nature of battle in the Great War that produced this 'demand' for a Eucharistic version of Christianity. Prost, in *Les Anciens Combattants et la Societé Française*, uses as base data 45 kilos of unedited *temoignages* of 425 French *Poilus* and produces a view of the actual experience of war.[1] One's own death was something which either happened or not—it was simply too quick and unpredictable to 'know'. Actually killing someone face to face, that is, the killing of a distinct human individual, was a rare experience, given the style and technology of war: 'in war, murdering someone is rare'.[2] (In Remarque's *All Quiet on the Western Front*, the truth of this analysis is borne out; the individual killing by stabbing of a French soldier in the shell hole is the worst killing; and at the end the last German boy-soldier dies, by sniper, while reaching out for a butterfly). Prost writes:

> War as really experienced is being with death in all its forms. Soldiers lived for entire days or even weeks in a kind of neighbourliness or intimacy with death.[3]

He quotes Norton Cru—'it was with our flesh that we knew war'[4]— and P. Cazin:

> I saw here, in the wood of Ailly, walls made of bodies. Rotting fingers stuck out, hurriedly covered with tar. There were scalps covered with a hideous moss, and feet everywhere—feet in boots, all plastered and twisted. And everywhere the terrible stench which made us blanch.[5]

Poetry (Harmondsworth: Penguin, 1981).

   1.   A. Prost, *Les anciens combattants et la societé française* (Paris: Presse de la Fondation Nationale des Sciences Politiques, 1977).
   2.   Prost, *Les anciens combattants*, p. 14.
   3.   Prost, *Les anciens combattants*, p. 6.
   4.   Prost, *Les anciens combattants*, p. 6.
   5.   Prost, *Les anciens combattants*, p. 7.

Prost quotes from men forced to listen helplessly to the screams and cries for help of men wounded and lying out in no-man's-land; and he asks:

> What can be said about this endless suffering of their fellow-soldiers to which the front-line troops were the helpless spectators? What could it have been like to see the man next to you in the trench in agony, crying out to you, floundering, calling out or with blood all over him—or else in silence staring at you, begging you for help which you both know is not available, or passing on to you his last, dying thoughts, savage in their simplicity—all this, an absolutely intolerable situation in which to be. . .
> In such a world it is entirely understandable that the soldiers had recourse to a terrible despairing beseeching, a kind of religious cry for help. . .
> They suffered, and they suffered without being able to do anything about it . . . In the literal sense of the word, they endured a Passion. No sense of shame, no reticence, no modesty would impel them to keep silent about what they had suffered. In the war they were the purely passive victims of a holocaust.[1]

Prost goes on to show how much of what the returning soldiers felt impelled to 'talk about' centred on the iconography and epigraphy of the war memorials. The war memorials, in France and in Britain, were how the war was talked about. They are the dancer and the dance, a sacred liturgical text summing up a history, insisting on remembrance, and marking out more potently than the Treaty of Rome or Hadrian's Wall the real, grim place of Christian Europe. War turns problems into tragedies; and as Prost shows, death in war stung very surely those who survived it.

The returning soldiers had to find some way of salvation, both for what they had done (that is, taken part in killing) and for what they had not done (that is, die). They had, at the behest of and on behalf of the civil society to which they were returning, transgressed a terrible taboo: 'I am,' said one nice old Polish Jewish airman to my students, 'a professional killer,'—and then he cried. War memorials are a text seeking forgiveness, a plea for reacceptance into the world of nonkilling, the world of innocence, including the innocence of those boys who went to war, some of whom came back—but without their innocence. Soldiers know that there is, ineluctably, no forgiveness for them; the taboo on killing is too strong, and civil society will always betray its defenders. The taboo has to be adamantly insisted upon

1. Prost, *Les anciens combattants*, pp. 9, 12, 14.

especially on those occasions—war—when necessity requires its transgression. War remembrance rituals are in essence therefore collusive and doomed attempts at mutual forgiving between those who asked for the killing to be carried out and those who did it. The story of the Cross suits this purpose, because it is in so many ways a story of innocent death, the death of a lamb, a story of voluntary, self-giving death, of the death of no one else, and of a death which forgives and saves everyone—even those who deny, and forget, and thereby betray. No doubt other cultures have their own way of addressing death in war. Europe's war memorials are its version of the Passion story of a young man and of those who died similarly.

'Memory and Monument':
Holocaust Testimony as Sacred Text

Isabel Wollaston

To refer to Holocaust testimony as 'sacred text' might seem excessive, but it was the belief that bearing witness was 'a sacred task' which inspired many of the victims to write.[1] Primo Levi went further and argued that such testimony should provide 'the stories of a new Bible'.[2] Today, few would challenge Jonathan Sacks's view that 'there is a religious duty to remember the Holocaust'.[3] Indeed, the situation is now such that Jacob Neusner argues that 'the myth of Holocaust and Redemption' has replaced the 'Dual Torah' as the dominant form of Judaism in Israel and the United States.[4]

It could be said that the issue is no longer whether Holocaust testimony is a sacred text, but rather how such testimony is to be interpreted. James Young suggests that one way of answering this question is by looking at Holocaust memorials: these 'memorial texts' give

1.   C. Kaplan, '31 July 1942', in *Scroll of Agony: A Diary of the Warsaw Ghetto* (trans. A. Katsh; London: Hamish Hamilton, 1966), p. 313.

2.   P. Levi, *If This Is A Man* (trans. S. Woolf; London: Abacus, 1987), p. 72. See also E. Wiesel, *Messengers of God* (trans. M. Wiesel; New York: Summit Books, 1976).

3.   J. Sacks, *Jewish Chronicle*, 16 June 1989.

4.   J. Neusner, *Stranger at Home: 'The Holocaust', Zionism, and American Judaism* (Chicago and London: Chicago University Press, 1981), and *Death and Birth of Judaism: The Impact of Christianity, Secularism, and the Holocaust on Jewish Faith* (New York: Basic Books, 1982). See also I. Jakobovits, 'Some Personal, Theological and Religious Responses to the Holocaust', *Holocaust and Genocide Studies* 3.4 (1988), pp. 371-81; I. Schorsch, 'The Holocaust and Jewish Survival', *Midstream* 27.1 (1981), pp. 38-42; D. Silver, 'Choose Life', *Judaism* 35.40 (1986), pp. 458-66; and M. Berenbaum, *After Tragedy and Triumph: Modern Jewish Thought and the American Experience* (Cambridge: Cambridge University Press, 1990), pp. 43-60, 126-33.

public expression to a variety of diverse, and even conflicting, interpretations of the Holocaust.[1] Given Lawrence Langer's insistence that
there is no one story of the event, but rather a multiplicity of stories,
we should not be surprised to find a similar diversity in the memorials
commemorating the event.[2] Those in Israel and Poland provide a case
in point. In Israel, remembrance of the Holocaust forms 'a critical
element in the public explanation of why there must be a State of
Israel'.[3] Although the victims are consistently described as 'Martyrs
and Heroes', there is an implicit emphasis on the latter. According to
the guide book to Yad Vashem (the national memorial to the
Holocaust), this is because there is an urgent need for 'it [to] be known
and comprehended, that the Jews were not only victims, they were
also among the victors'.[4] Thus, alongside memorials to the 'Martyrs',
there are others commemorating the 'Soldiers, Ghetto-Fighters and
Partisans'. By contrast, in Poland we find two distinct and contradictory interpretations of the Holocaust. On the one hand, there are state
memorials to Polish resistance and 'the martyrdom of the Polish and
other nations'.[5] On the other hand, there are Jewish memorials to the
almost total annihilation of Polish Jewry.

The purpose of this paper is twofold: first, to offer a brief summary
of the ways in which Holocaust testimony is understood as sacred text,
and secondly, to consider the ways in which these interpretations are
reflected in memorials, specifically those in Poland.

1.   J. Young, 'The Texture of Memory: Holocaust Memorials and their
Meaning', *Dimensions* 3.2 (1988), pp. 4-8. See also *idem*, the last chapter in
*Writing and Rewriting the Holocaust: Narrative and the Consequences of
Interpretation* (Bloomington: Indiana University Press, 1988); 'Memory and
Monument', in G. Hartman (ed.), *Bitburg in Moral and Political Perspective*
(Bloomington: Indiana University Press, 1986), pp. 103-13; 'The Biography of a
Memorial Icon: Nathan Rapoport's Warsaw Ghetto Monument', *Representations* 26
(1989), pp. 69-106; 'Holocaust Memorials: The Art of Memory, the Permanence of
Monuments', *Journal of Art* (February 1990).

2.   L. Langer, *Versions of Survival: The Holocaust and the Human Spirit*
(Albany, NY: State University of New York Press, 1982). See also *idem*, *Holocaust
Testimonies: The Ruins of Memory* (New Haven and London: Yale University
Press, 1991).

3.   Neusner, *Stranger at Home*, p. 88.

4.   R. Dafni (ed.), *Yad Vashem: The Holocaust Martyrs' and Heroes'
Remembrance Authority, Jerusalem* (Jerusalem: Yad Vashem, 1986), p. 18.

5.   This phrase is found on the inscription on the memorial at Maidanek.

Menahem Kon, co-founder of *Oneg Shabbat* (the Warsaw Ghetto underground archive) spoke for many: 'I consider it a sacred duty to write all I know'.[1] The Jews in the ghettos and camps were acutely conscious of the Nazis' desire 'to erase all traces of their savage deed and to ensure that no one will remain to tell of it, to describe the act'.[2] In Himmler's words, the extermination of Europe's Jews would remain a 'glorious never-to-be-written page' in German history. As a result, this period can be interpreted as 'a war against memory',[3] a struggle to see *who* would write the history of this period, or whether it would be written at all; the Nazis were determined to leave no trace, whereas their victims were determined to write 'a luminous page in the dark history of our times'.[4] Tadeusz Borowski expresses the victims' fear: 'If the Germans win the war, what will the world know about us?'[5] By often quite literally burying their testimony, those who died preserved the 'scorched vestiges' of their own passing.[6] Thus, testimony served two functions. First, it was 'an act of war against fascism'.[7] For Emmanuel Ringelblum, testimony struck the enemy 'a mighty blow', revealing that which was meant to be kept secret.[8] Secondly, testimony would provide 'source material' for the poets, elegists and historians of the future, thus preserving the memory of those who died.[9]

In one sense at least, the victims discharged their 'sacred duty': this page of history *has* been written. The responsibility for preserving the memory of the dead now lies with the survivors and the community as

1.   Menahem Kon, '15 November 1942', in J. Kermish (ed.), *To Live with Honor and Die with Honor! Selected Documents from the Warsaw Ghetto Underground Archives 'O.S.' ['Oneg Shabbath']* (Jerusalem: Yad Vashem, 1986), p. 56.

2.   Kon, '15 November 1942', p. 23.

3.   P. Levi, *The Drowned and the Saved* (trans. R. Rosenthal; London: Michael Joseph, 1988), p. 18.

4.   Kon, '15 November 1942', p. 24.

5.   T. Borowski, *This Way for the Gas, Ladies and Gentlemen* (trans. B. Vedder; New York: Penguin Books, 1976), p. 132.

6.   E. Wiesel, *One Generation After* (trans. L. Edelman and E. Wiesel; New York: Schocken Books, 1982), p. 39.

7.   Levi, *The Drowned and the Saved*, p. 7.

8.   E. Ringelblum, '26 June 1942', in Kermish (ed.), *To Live with Honor and Die with Honor!*, p. 34.

9.   Kaplan, '18 January 1940', in *Scroll of Agony*, p. 86.

a whole. According to Wiesel, 'anyone who does not commit themselves to active remembering is an accomplice of the executioner, for
he betrays the dead by forgetting them'.[1]

Emil Fackenheim elevates such a claim to the status of an additional,
614th Commandment: to forget 'the Martyrs of the Holocaust' is to
hand Hitler 'a posthumous victory'.[2] Neusner suggests that
Fackenheim should be seen as one of the architects of a new Judaism
of 'Holocaust and Redemption', in which the Holocaust and the State
of Israel become a 'myth' providing 'a transcendent perspective on
events... a story lending meaning and importing sanctity to ordinary,
everyday actions—a new religious affirmation'.[3] The Holocaust
provides an answer to the question, 'Why be Jewish?': 'because you
have no choice'.[4] In the aftermath of the Holocaust, when one out of
three Jews was killed, including 80 per cent of all Jewish rabbis and
scholars, the state of Israel becomes 'a metaphysical necessity'.[5] To
challenge this 'myth' or, more precisely, to question the uniqueness of
the Holocaust or the policies of the state of Israel, is 'the fundamental
heresy'.[6] According to Neusner, 'the myth of Holocaust and
Redemption' is now the dominant form of Judaism in Israel and the
United States. In many ways, the 1953 'Martyrs and Heroes
Remembrance Law' gives symbolic expression to this 'myth' in its
provision for conferring 'commemorative citizenship of the state of
Israel' upon the six million victims of the Holocaust as 'a token of
their having been gathered to their people'.[7]

Unfortunately, not only have the victims' hopes been fulfilled, some
of their fears have also proved justified. The desire to testify sprang,

1. E. Wiesel, 'Art and Culture After the Holocaust', in E. Fleischner (ed.),
Auschwitz: Beginning of a New Era? (New York: Ktav, 1977), pp. 403-15, 409.
2. E. Fackenheim, 'Jewish Values in the Post-Holocaust Future', *Judaism* 16.3
(1967), pp. 266-99, 273. Fackenheim subsequently challenges the application of the
label 'Martyrs' to the victims of the Holocaust, given that they had no choice,
whereas in the past the option of conversion was available as an alternative to martyrdom. See E. Fackenheim, *The Jewish Return into History* (New York: Schocken
Books, 1978), pp. 234-51.
3. Neusner, *Stranger at Home*, pp. 65-66.
4. Neusner, *Death and Birth of Judaism*, p. 281.
5. Neusner, *Death and Birth of Judaism*, p. 269. The figures are those of
Berenbaum in *After Tragedy and Triumph*, p. 70.
6. Berenbaum, *After Tragedy and Triumph*, p. 83.
7. Dafni (ed.), *Yad Vashem*, p. 5.

in part, from the fear that no one would live to tell the tale, or that those who came after would be unable to appreciate what the victims' life—and death—had been like. Testifying after the event, survivors question their ability to communicate their experience, or insist that this experience only constitutes a fraction of the whole. Primo Levi spoke of survivor-testimony as 'the story of things seen from close by, not experienced personally'.[1] The 'sacred duty' of the survivor is not confined to bearing witness, it includes acting as mediator and custodian to the memory of the dead. However, is it possible to discharge such a duty? Sidra Ezrahi suggests that it is not: the survivors are attempting 'to put the pages of the book back together'.[2] In bearing witness to the past, they illustrate how much of that past has been lost. For example, Wiesel notes that the *shtetl*-culture of Eastern Europe can now be found 'only in words, in words alone'.[3] Langer speaks of survivors' 'anguished memory'—their consciousness of 'a lost piece of the past that can be evoked but nor restored'.[4] For Wiesel, testimony and writing serve as a symbolic 'tombstone' to the dead.[5] Through testifying, he attempts 'to recreate a vanished universe. . . to bring back at least for a while some of the men and women the killers robbed of their lives and their names'.[6] For Levi, testimony preserves the memory of the dead by offering them 'the ambiguous perennial existence of literary characters'.[7] Both survivors are struggling to fulfil their 'sacred duty' by rehumanizing the abstract figure of 'six million', and thus preserving the memory of the individuals who died.

Jewish Holocaust memorials in Poland serve a similar function. Young notes that Polish Jews often only 'returned to their homes long enough to erect memorials to their lost families and communities before moving on'.[8] This compulsion to erect memorials arises from

1. Levi, *The Drowned and the Saved*, p. 64.
2. S. Ezrahi, *By Words Alone: The Holocaust in Literature* (Chicago: University of Chicago Press, 1980), p. 110.
3. Wiesel, 'Art and Culture after the Holocaust', p. 411.
4. Langer, *Holocaust Testimonies*, p. 52.
5. E. Wiesel, *Legends of Our Time* (trans. S. Donadio; New York: Schocken Books, 1982), pp. 8-10.
6. E. Wiesel, 'A Personal Response', *Face to Face* 6 (1979), pp. 35-37.
7. P. Levi, *Moments of Reprieve* (trans. R. Feldman; London: Abacus, 1987), pp. 9-10.
8. J. Young, 'Museums and Memorial Institutes: A General Survey', in *Encyclopedia of the Holocaust*, III (New York: Macmillan, 1990), pp. 1010-12.

the desire 'to produce something concrete to commemorate a world that has disappeared. . . as an inadequate response to an overpowering sense of loss'.[1] Broken tombstones provide one of the dominant memorial motifs: Jewish memorials are often constructed from the broken fragments of tombstones vandalized by the Nazis. Young suggests that such memorials symbolically incorporate 'and thereby preserve. . . the irreparable break in the continuity of Jewish life and memory in Poland'.[2]

The Jewish memory of the Holocaust differs markedly from that of the wider Polish community; the memorials constructed by the latter are 'governed by different memories of the same events'.[3] The suffering of the Jews becomes a part of 'the martyrdom of the Polish nation': 'The three million Polish Jews now all become Poles, and when added to the three million Polish victims of the Nazis, make up the total of *six million Poles*—victims of *genocide*'.[4] The Holocaust becomes a *shared* experience. As a result, 'martyrology' and 'survival' are no longer descriptions applicable only to the experience of the Jews. Holocaust testimony is seen to bear witness to the *actual* fate of the Jews and the *potential* fate of the Poles.

Problems inevitably arise when this interpretation of events is challenged by the very 'different memories' of the Jews, or the revisionist approach of Communist historiography. For obvious reasons, the latter's concern was to attribute all successful resistance to the Communist underground, while accusing the larger—and anti-Communist—Home Army of anti-Semitism and collaboration with the Nazis. Thus, while Jews are sensitive to the 'Polonization' of the Holocaust, Poles are sensitive to accusations of collaboration or any minimization of their suffering under the Nazis. The recurrent disputes over the Holocaust in Poland can be seen as the collision of two—possibly three—'myths' (in Neusner's sense of the word). The controversy generated by, for example, Claude Lanzmann's film *Shoah*, Jan Błoński's article, 'The Poor Poles Look at the Ghetto', or the Carmelite convent at Auschwitz, illustrates the tensions existing

1.   Berenbaum, *After Tragedy and Triumph*, p. 50.
2.   Young, 'The Texture of Memory', p. 5. See also R. Wisse, 'Poland's Jewish Ghosts', *Commentary* 83.1 (1987), pp. 25-33.
3.   Wisse, 'Poland's Jewish Ghosts', p. 26.
4.   I. Irwin-Zarecka, *Neutralizing Memory: The Jew in Contemporary Poland* (New Brunswick and Oxford: Transaction Publishers, 1989), p. 62.

between Polish and Jewish 'mythical' readings of the Holocaust.

The differences between these two 'myths' can best be illustrated by presenting each in its most extreme form. From a Jewish perspective, Poland is 'a forsaken place where Jewish culture flourished long ago, then it got worse and worse, and it all ended in tragedy, and there is now only a painful absence'.[1] The Polish population are accused of regarding Jewish suffering with either indifference or tacit approval. This indifference is then compounded by 'a kind of retroactive genocide': the dead are killed a second time when the specificity of their fate is denied.[2] Thus, Polish memorials to the Holocaust are held to ignore the Jewish identity of the victims—they are as *Judenrein* as the country in which they stand. To take but one example: in 1967, the 'International Monument to the Victims of Fascism' was erected at Auschwitz–Birkenau. The only suggestion that Jews were among these victims is found in the inclusion of Hebrew and Yiddish among the 19 languages used for the inscription.[3]

The monument at Auschwitz–Birkenau illustrates the tension existing between Jewish and Polish memory. The latter emphasizes the population's heroic struggle against Fascism. Pride of place is given to the Nazi campaign against the Polish elite, symbolized by the opening of the Auschwitz concentration camp in June 1940. Thus, Auschwitz is seen as both the 'symbol of martyrdom and extermination which affected the majority of families';[4] and 'a shrine visited annually by hundreds of thousands of Polish mourners'.[5] Poles see themselves as the primary victims of World War II, the experience of which served to give further credence to the romantic myth of Poland as 'the Christ of the Nations'. Stanislaw Krajewski summarizes this perspective and indicates the nature of the problems it poses: 'Poles perceive themselves as victims of history. They cannot tolerate the thought that someone else might have suffered even more. It is they who are victims and that is the end of the argument. So, firstly, Jews could not

1. S. Krajewski, quoted in A. Bryk, 'Poland and the Memory of the Holocaust', *Partisan Review* 57.2 (1990), pp. 228-38.

2. R. Wisse, 'Poland Without Jews', *Commentary* 66.2 (1978), pp. 64-67.

3. Young, 'Memory and Monument', p. 106. See also *idem*, 'The Texture of Memory', pp. 4-6; and J. Webber's paper in this volume.

4. Cardinal Macharski, quoted in W.T. Bartoszewski, *The Convent at Auschwitz* (London: Bowerdean Press, 1990), p. 32.

5. Wisse, 'Poland's Jewish Ghosts', p. 28.

have suffered more than we did, and secondly, we could not have added to their suffering, because a victim cannot cause suffering to others'.[1] He suggests that anti-Semitism in Poland should be seen as the inevitable result of the conflict of two sacred myths: 'there is no room for *two* chosen nations in the same land'.[2]

This necessarily brief sketch of the differing interpretations of the Holocaust in Poland indicates that it is not sufficient to regard the subject as 'a sacred realm', and to assume that the parameters of this realm are universally agreed upon.[3] Even if Holocaust testimony is popularly regarded as sacred text, there is no—or only a partial—consensus as to how it should be interpreted. Many of the controversies generated by Holocaust memorials are fuelled by an inability to recognize the existence, let alone the legitimacy, of interpretations other than one's own. Perhaps it should come as no surprise to find that the stories of this 'new Bible' are as open to interpretation, and as much a source of impassioned controversy, as those of Scripture.

1.   S. Krajewski, quoted in A. Polonsky (ed.), *My Brother's Keeper? Recent Polish Debates on the Holocaust* (London: Routledge, 1990), pp. 102-103.
2.   Krajewski, in Polonsky (ed.), *My Brother's Keeper?*, pp. 102-103.
3.   The description of the Holocaust as 'a sacred realm' is by E. Wiesel, quoted in I. Abrahamson (ed.), *Against Silence: The Voice and Vision of Elie Wiesel*, I (New York: Holocaust Library, 1985), p. 190.

Creating a New Inscription for the Memorial at Auschwitz–Birkenau: A Short Chapter in the Mythologization of the Holocaust[*]

Jonathan Webber

The purpose of this paper is to offer a contribution to the study of vernacular sacred texts. By 'vernacular' I am referring to texts which are part of the everyday experience of society, as opposed to classical sacred texts, usually associated with scripturally based religions, which are usually in the hands of an educated literate elite. Vernacular sacred texts are those which are found, for example, as inscriptions on public monuments such as war memorials or foundation stones of buildings. Such inscriptions are 'sacred' in the sense that they relate to major cultural or social issues—but they do so in a summary, or simplified form, unlike the obviously much more elaborate types of literary structures typical of classical scriptural texts. What vernacular texts have in common with scriptural texts is that they are both underpinned, or indeed generated, by myth. Myth in this sense is to be understood not in the ordinary conversational or colloquial use of the term to mean something untrue or false, but—following anthropological usage—as referring to something which society members believe to be true, whether or not the events or ideas represented in them are in fact true. Using this definition of myth, both vernacular texts and scriptural texts can be said to be the public

*   I should like to express my thanks to Isabel Wollaston, who encouraged me to write this paper, and to the staff of the Auschwitz State Museum who assisted me in many ways during the course of the anthropological fieldwork I conducted at Auschwitz over several months during the summers of 1988–91. The Auschwitz data discussed in this paper are all drawn from observations made during this fieldwork, internal reports and memos to which the Museum kindly lent me access, and the proceedings of the International Auschwitz Council. I am grateful also to Connie Wilsack for perceptive editorial comments.

expression of fundamental cultural preoccupations that can be found within a given society. The subject of Auschwitz—and in particular the nature of public inscriptions to be found on the site today—offers an interesting opportunity for the elaboration of these themes.

I

Let me begin this paper with a short historical narrative. Since 1989 the Polish government has taken a serious interest in the whole question of the future of Auschwitz.[1] This interest was partly due to the controversy over the Carmelite convent, which came to a head in that year.[2] It was partly due to the end of socialist government, also in the summer of 1989. And it was also partly due to a desire to re-establish relations—political, intellectual and economic—with Israel and diaspora Jewish communities. Thus it was that in 1989 the Polish government put out feelers to find ways in which Jewish intellectual

---

1.   There are complex terminological difficulties surrounding precisely what is meant by 'Auschwitz', and usages differ. Strictly speaking, Auschwitz comprised a series of some 40 concentration camps, administered from a base camp itself surrounded by a special zone of about 15 square miles that lay immediately to the west and south-west of the town of Oświecim (which was itself renamed Auschwitz by the Germans). Today, however, the topographic reference has shrunk: 'Auschwitz' is commonly used to refer only to specific parts of this complex, i.e. those parts that have in effect come to be seen topographically as symbolic of the horrors perpetrated. In some usages this means the base camp (and occasionally also certain buildings in its immediate vicinity, such as the building in which the Carmelite convent is located). In other usages it means the extension two miles away at Birkenau (where the principal apparatus of mass murder—i.e. gas chambers and crematoria—were located). And in yet other usages (as in this paper, for example), Auschwitz means both places taken together (with or without the intervening terrain), whether or not a specific topographic reference is intended. It is in Birkenau, referred to in this paper as Auschwitz–Birkenau, that the main Auschwitz monument (the subject of this paper) was constructed.
2.   On this controversy four books have so far appeared, itself a representative fact suggestive of the controversy as a historical event: W.T. Bartoszewski, *The Convent at Auschwitz* (London: Bowerdean Press, 1990); S. Chomet, *Outrage at Auschwitz* (London: Newman-Hemisphere, 1990); T. Klein, *L'Affaire du Carmel d'Auschwitz* (Paris: Jacques Bertoin, 1991); and C. Rittner and J.K. Roth (eds.), *Memory Offended: The Auschwitz Convent Controversy* (New York: Praeger, 1991). Klein's book is of particular interest, given his role as a principal Jewish negotiator in the bilateral discussions with the church authorities.

and possibly financial input could be made with regard to Auschwitz, culminating in the establishment of an International Auschwitz Council. I was invited to become a founder member of this body.

At its first meeting, held in June 1990, one of the many problems discussed was the issue of what sort of new text could be proposed for the inscription at the main international monument at Auschwitz–Birkenau. The original inscription—a simple dedication, repeated in 19 different languages on individual plaques, to the memory of the four million men, women and children who died in Auschwitz between 1940 and 1945—had been removed on the order of the director of the Auschwitz Museum in the early part of 1990, when it was finally decided to recognize that the figure of four million which had been mentioned on the inscription did not correspond with the figure for the total number of Auschwitz victims agreed by internationally respected historians. Western historians think that a more accurate figure is less than two million, probably in the order of 1.3–1.5 million, although it is unlikely that the exact figure will ever be known.[1] Regardless of the historical controversies, however, the question the Council had to resolve was how to word the new inscription, and on this three opinions emerged.

The first was that the monument should bear some historical information, for example: 'To the memory of the enormous and unknown numbers of victims, largely Jewish, of the Nazi war machine 1940–1945'. In other words, the new inscription would remove the problem of specifying the precise number of victims, but would also include a reference (for the first time) to the fact that the overwhelming majority—historians think that it is probably in the region of 90 per cent—were Jewish. In discussion of this approach, the Council went into a considerable amount of detail as to whether or not Gypsies should be mentioned, alongside Jews; whether Poles should be specifically referred to, alongside Jews and Gypsies; whether reference should be made to Soviet prisoners of war, who were murdered there in great numbers; and so on. It became clear that to compress reference to all the different groups of victims within the space of a single inscription that would at the same time be meaningful

---

1. For a detailed recent study see F. Piper, 'Estimating the Number of Deportees to and Victims of the Auschwitz–Birkenau Camp', *Yad Vashem Studies* 21 (1991), pp. 49-103. The author is the head of the historical department of the Auschwitz State Museum.

and small enough to fit into the space available on the monument was going to be a very difficult task; yet the danger was that any new inscription would not be sufficiently inclusive to cover all relevant interest groups. Adding the reference to Jews was an innovation that was welcomed, in the interests of (post-communist) historical truth— but omitting other groups would represent a new set of historical distortions. The problem was debated at some length by the Council in attempting to reach a consensus.

Hence the appeal of the second approach to this subject, namely to have no historical information on the inscription at all, but to have something more poetic. It was suggested that a verse be used from the book of Job (16.18): 'O Earth cover not up my blood and let my cry never cease'. Underlying this proposal was the implication that it was unnecessary to rehearse all that Auschwitz stood for, because visitors to the place would, presumably, already know something about the historical experience that Auschwitz represented, without having to have it all explained on an inscription. Historical details could be supplied elsewhere, for example in the official museum guide book. According to this view, therefore, an inscription on the main monument should restrict itself to something a little more contemplative and reflective—to provide a mood for the visitor, rather than a record of a historical event.

However, there was a third school of thought: to have both types of inscription—both historical information and something more meditative and reflective. This was not merely a compromise: it reflected the view that what Auschwitz means, what needs to be said today at Auschwitz, about Auschwitz, was precisely the conjunction between information and contemplation, between fact and emotion.

Listening to these discussions (much of which was quite agonized as far as the details were concerned), I slowly became aware that what I was witnessing was precisely the creation of a modern vernacular sacred text: how to articulate the elements of what may be considered a key modern myth.

This paper should thus be read together with the paper by Jon Davies about war memorials.[1] To adapt Davies' principal arguments: the new text at Auschwitz–Birkenau should be something which is easily understood; it should require no explanation, and certainly no

1.   Reproduced in this volume.

footnotes or other scholarly apparatus; it should not exhibit any critical reading of the historical material it was to commemorate, but should state its points clearly and unambiguously. The inscription should be formulaic, it should somehow have an aura about itself of being hallowed; and in this way it should constitute a symbol, a linguistic symbol, for the meaning of the place. The inscription would probably be read and photographed by countless millions of future visitors to the place; services of commemoration would be held adjacent to it. The text would in this way, one could say, recall a folk-European memory of what happened in Auschwitz. Indeed, as I would prefer to say, it would *constitute* a folk-European memory of the place and the event. In short, the inscription would signify its own contribution as to how Auschwitz is to be remembered in the future.

What the Council was, in effect, confronted with in trying to formulate the actual text of the new inscription was the task of defining a myth, a sacred tale, of Auschwitz. For what the Auschwitz–Birkenau memorial would 'say' would in this sense be a vernacular sacred text, its sacredness both reflecting and evoking a tabooed, untouchable domain: Auschwitz not only as human catastrophe, but as an insoluble riddle, the reality of its existence ever to be agonized over as a key problem and preoccupation of European society and of others the world over.[1]

1.   Representations of a myth take time to evolve, and, as will be argued below, they need to take account of competing formulations. The process is inevitably time-consuming, a fact which contributes to the sense of agony—not to mention the concomitant, contradictory feelings of urgency and importance—which have characterized the debate. Since this paper was given (July 1991), the Council has held a series of further meetings and considered reports of a sub-committee that was established to deal with the matter. Although this issue has now dominated the agenda for several meetings of the Council, no final, comprehensive solution has been found (although there has been a strengthening of the resolve to try to deal with the problem). The mood of the meetings has shifted towards what I have termed the third school of thought, that is, an approach which at one level is more inclusive than the other two proposals. In that sense it is not surprising that the discussion has also extended itself outwards to the whole issue of informational and commemorative inscriptions in Auschwitz–Birkenau generally.

As of today (March 1993) the problem is still not resolved completely. At its most recent meeting, in January 1993, the Council agreed to a solution proposing not one inscription but two: a 'main' inscription in four languages (Polish, Hebrew, English, and a Gypsy language—although some council members believe that a fifth language, Yiddish, should also appear), and a different, albeit similar, text in 19

II

One of the central features of a sacred tale is that it contains internal contradictions. It is quite likely that it is this very potential for conveying or incorporating multiple meanings that makes it possible for a sacred tale or a sacred text, be it scriptural or vernacular, to carry authority over time. Circumstances change, but the text remains changeless, as it stands, for ever, brooding over the generations as they come and go. Scholars analysing the sacred texts of the Bible have preferred to resolve the problem of internal contradictions by postulating their multiple authorship. But from the point of view of the believer, the multiple meanings of the text are what is striking. Balaam, for example, is represented in the biblical text both as an outstanding prophet and as a model of the truly wicked person.[1] How is it possible for Balaam to represent both kinds of figure simultaneously? For the scholar the answer probably is that there are two different traditions about Balaam which have been incorporated into the single version of the Bible as transmitted to us today. For the believer, on the other hand, it is this very equivocal character of Balaam which makes the story of Balaam worthy of incorporation in the text at all, inasmuch as it represents a typical biblical paradox on which the believer is to meditate.

A similar structure can be observed with regard to the formation and self-expression of the contemporary Auschwitz myth: what

languages for the existing individual plaques alongside. Which 19 languages, or the order in which they will appear, was not resolved at this meeting, however. Theoretically, the languages of the main inscription should reflect the languages of the contemporary visitor, whereas the languages represented on the 19 plaques notionally signify the languages of the victims. The distinction is, in principle, a good one, but the fit is inexact: how many 'languages' were spoken by the Yugoslavs who died in Auschwitz? In what sense does the Hebrew language fairly represent the ordinary speech of the European Jewish victims? The asymmetrical nature of these examples illustrates the considerable difficulty people have today in attempting not only to identify a precise set of meanings Auschwitz has or ought to have, but also to compress those meanings into a single unambiguous formula.

1.   The story of Balaam, at Num. 22.4, is commented on at Mic. 6.4-5 (where his greatness is ranked alongside that of Moses, Aaron and Miriam). Num. 31.8 and 16 record, however, his death at the hands of the Israelites and the accusation that he brought disaster on the people; Deut. 23.4-7 completely reduces him to the rank of villain.

Auschwitz is presumed to signify turns out, on closer inspection, to be saturated with internal contradictions of many kinds. Let me give some examples, though for the sake of brevity I shall not be able to do much more than mention the sort of things that I have in mind.

Auschwitz is a cemetery, inasmuch as the site contains the ashes of countless or indefinitely large numbers of its victims—their ashes are buried in the fields round about, and in that sense their remains can be said to be present in the place. So Auschwitz is clearly in one sense a cemetery. On the other hand, Auschwitz is the very opposite of a cemetery. A cemetery is usually a place which has been specifically consecrated by a religious or other group, for the purpose of interring the remains of its members. It is hallowed ground, sacralized in advance of people being buried there, and a ceremony is usually carried out when funerals actually take place. Auschwitz has none of these features. The people who are 'buried' there were not buried in any formal sense of the term. Indeed, the disposal of their bodies was the very opposite of burial, having been done totally unceremoniously and unceremonially. There is no sense in which one can say that the site was hallowed or consecrated in advance for the respectful and dignified interment of its victims. The first contradiction, therefore, is that Auschwitz is both a cemetery and not a cemetery at the same time.

However, whatever can be said about Auschwitz in relation to the category of cemetery, today it is primarily a museum. The museum was established at the order of the Polish government shortly after the war, in 1947, and was designated as a historical site to be preserved for eternity. Today 175 people or so are employed by the museum, and there are approximately 750,000 visitors every year (1990 figures). The Auschwitz State Museum has the full trappings of a museum: a director and an assistant director; several departments, including a historical department, an educational department, a publications department, and so on; it produces an annual report; it survives on an annual budget approved by the Ministry of Culture. It has, as every museum would have, a set of guides, both licensed and unlicensed, and of course an official guide book.

In addition to being a museum, however, Auschwitz is also a memorial site—a place set aside to commemorate a historical event— so it is no ordinary museum. It is a rather special kind of museum, perhaps analogous in this sense to a historical museum at the site of a famous battle, such as the Battle of Waterloo. And, being a memorial site, it therefore has monuments, such as the main monument at Auschwitz–Birkenau to which I have referred above, although there are a number of other, smaller monuments dotted about the site.

Fourthly, Auschwitz is a major tourist site, attracting tourists from nearly every country in the world; and the visit to Auschwitz is widely advertised in Poland by the tourist agencies. There is a substantial car park for coaches and private cars. There is a hotel, a restaurant, a souvenir shop, a bookshop, a left-luggage counter, a series of public lavatories, and so on. A wide variety of postcards are available, as well as slides and other such materials.

In addition to all this, Auschwitz should be regarded as a pilgrimage site. Indeed, there is a flower shop at the entrance to the museum—a very unusual thing to have in a museum, but those tourists who would prefer perhaps in some sense to regard themselves as pilgrims are often to be seen purchasing flowers and placing them in unexpected corners, both inside and outside the barracks, adjacent to the museum exhibits or in the open fields—sometimes by the ruins of the crematoria and gas chambers. Jewish visitors often light memorial candles in some of these places. Auschwitz as a pilgrimage site needs to be understood as possessing its own sociology, distinct from the other types that I have already mentioned. For example, it attracts organized groups of Christian or Jewish youth from a number of countries, including Poland, Germany and Israel; such groups often have a programme of special lectures, seminars or prayer metings more typical of pilgrims than of the ordinary secular visitor. They thereby encourage, at Auschwitz, a sense of place reminiscent of the sacred shrines more usually associated with pilgrimage sites.

How can Auschwitz be all these things at once? The point is that it is precisely all these things at once. Its essential nature today is that it possesses a series of internal contradictions, each element of which, though true in its own way, is not exhaustive of the truth.

In addition to these contradictions one can propose a series of other contradictions as well. The meaning of Auschwitz must obviously be connected with its historical past. But I suspect that the attribution of meaning which visitors place on the site is much more usually directed towards its present meanings, not its past meanings. For example, many of those Jews who treat the visit to Auschwitz as a kind of pilgrimage see the place as representing the ultimate disaster of diaspora

Jewish life and consequently as representing the decisive proof for the need for the state of Israel. But there are other meanings as well: the evil of Fascism, the evil of Nazism in particular, the death of God, the nature of the murderers' mentality, the truth of our own values. Some of these meanings are connected with the past, but some of them are clearly concerned with present preoccupations. It is natural, of course, for history to be rewritten in every generation according to contemporary values and preoccupations. In the case of Auschwitz the process is quite clear. History in this sense is being used as a backdrop, as a context, if not also a pretext, for contemplating present-day problems. Or, perhaps, one can suggest that Auschwitz is about 'them'— others, Nazis, Fascists, the Europe of 'The Past'—as opposed to ourselves. At a wider level still, one can discern yet other sets of contradictions: Auschwitz is full of meaning, full of meanings; but on the other hand it is totally devoid of meanings, is totally devoid of meaning. For some Orthodox Jews there is no theological significance to the Holocaust at all; it is its fundamental meaninglessness—to put the point in an extreme form—which is what the Holocaust is all about. Auschwitz somehow belongs to all humanity, for by definition there can be no one group to whom it actually belongs, whether this be Poles or Jews or Gypsies; on the other hand, Auschwitz is an empty place—it belongs to nobody. Auschwitz is a physical space which you can plot on a map, a map of Poland, a map of the city of Oświecim; but Auschwitz has got nothing to do with physical space, Auschwitz is a symbolic space. Finally, and this is by no means an exhaustive list,[1] Auschwitz is a place which for some is fundamentally perceived as a lonely field—it should be left alone. For others, however, Auschwitz is a place that everyone should come to, and when the visitor gets there, the more crowds the visitor sees in the place the better it is, because more people are taking in the message. The victims did not die in vain.

---

1.   This paper is thus to be taken as a preliminary set of suggestions which will form the basis of a larger work on the subject (though the interested reader may wish to consult my pamphlet, *The Future of Auschwitz: Some Personal Reflections* [Oxford: Oxford Centre for Postgraduate Hebrew Studies, 1992]).

III

Looking over this series of polarities or contradictions, one can only conclude that all the positions are valid; some more clearly so than others, perhaps, but nevertheless all equally valid in some sense or another. What makes this place mythological is precisely its lack of a single clear meaning, its capacity to sustain contradictions of many kinds, contradictions which are not trivial but are, on the contrary, of major significance. It is this capacity which provides the fundamental input that renders Auschwitz suitable for mythologization, and indeed expresses it.

The practical, albeit implicit, question facing the International Council was this: how to unpack all this onto an inscription for the monument at Auschwitz–Birkenau so as to create a formula that would be hallowed, easily understood, not suggestive of any critical readings, and would contribute a bona fide folk memory of the place? Well, nobody really knew, of course. But then the discourse about Auschwitz is in any case problematic. If you speak about the place too emotionally, then you're unfit for the discourse because you lack sufficient objectivity. If you speak about it too unemotionally, then you're also unfit to talk about it, because you haven't really absorbed its ultimate meanings.

Point for point, what I have been suggesting here about Auschwitz can be traced with regard to Jewish perceptions of the Holocaust itself. Jewish perceptions of the Holocaust today are so deeply contradictory that the very phenomenon has become mythologized—in much the same way that Auschwitz itself has become mythologized—through contradictory slogans, stereotypes and generalizations. The Holocaust itself, in the way that it is treated publicly—for example on inscriptions, in synagogues and elsewhere—has developed mythological features that are quite striking. Leading the way is the very taboo on whole parts of the subject, suggestive of the creation of a modern myth. For twenty years after the war, the Holocaust was hardly spoken about at all. Survivors wanted to forget, were often made to feel ashamed of having survived and instead felt that their duty was to put the whole subject behind them and start a new life. Today, on the other hand, the slogan is the reverse. Indeed, the single word 'Remember!' (or in Hebrew *zachor*) is the principal slogan that Jewish institutions, congregations, student bodies, youth groups and other organizations will usually propose in relation to the Holocaust. Yet, despite the conviction of Jewish people that the Holocaust is of paramount importance to them, they appear to have only the most fragmentary knowledge of it. The assumption is that academic specialists will somehow know all the details for them and arrange to keep them stored—a process reminiscent of how sacred scriptural texts are treated by the mass of believers. Jews have what can be called a liturgy of familiar words, familiar names, familiar photographs, familiar selected facts that together pass for knowledge of the Holocaust, that somehow are supposed to act as symbolic or metonymic of the whole. They do not remember even the names of all the major concentration camps. Bełżec, for example, has been almost completely forgotten in the popular Jewish imagination, even though as many as 600,000 Jews are thought to have been murdered there.[1] And then there are the contradictions: the view that the Holocaust is central to modern Jewish identity against the view that the Holocaust is a Gentile problem and has nothing to do with contemporary Jews or Judaism. Auschwitz ought somehow to be preserved, but at the same time the feeling is that the Jewish tradition does not venerate holy places (at least, not outside the Holy Land). Should the ruins of the gas chambers be preserved? No—let them fall down. Should the ruins of the gas chambers be preserved? Yes—a glass dome should be built over them to preserve them to show future generations, revisionists and others, what really happened. In short, the meaning of the Holocaust, the meaning of Auschwitz, is not at all obvious. This is why both the category, as well as the empirical details, have the potential for becoming mythologized.

The literary structure of a myth (such as the Bible, or modern perceptions of the Holocaust) is made up of the intermingling of moral observations and small details of historical narrative. Sometimes the narrative is not arranged sequentially—the details that are supplied are obviously presented as symbolic rather than as contributing to a full description of the whole. The details usually depend on different criteria for selection—in some cases they could be

1. See for example M. Gilbert, *The Holocaust: The Jewish Tragedy* (London: Collins, 1986), p. 502. It remains to be seen whether Holocaust historians will feel the need to revise the figures for Bełżec, Treblinka, Sobibór and other camps, given the general renewal of interest in the whole subject following the revision of the Auschwitz figures (see earlier footnote).

merely anecdotal, in other cases they could be exhaustive of the subject being described. The most important thing about them is that although they purport to represent a description (and an implicit theory) of the phenomenon in question, in practice they are not amenable to alternative discussion or rational debate. It would seem that it is this feature which is typical both of Auschwitz and of the developing Jewish perception of the Holocaust. The forgetting of Bełżec does not signify a failure to take the Holocaust seriously; on the contrary, that 'detail' is merely unnecessary in the construction of a mythologized view of the Holocaust.

There is no closed canon of meanings that can be attributed to the formulation of a sacred text or a corpus thereof; this is also the case with regard to Auschwitz. Some meanings are more 'meaningful' than others; some details are taken as more symbolic than others. What we are witnessing today, then, is a rare example of the opportunity to observe something that is in the process of becoming a myth. In one of the most remarkable mythological inversions that characterize this mode of thinking, Poles are substituted for Germans. It was the Poles, according to conventional Jewish beliefs today, who were responsible for the Holocaust. Auschwitz is in Poland—so the 'logic' runs—and Poles have always been anti-Semites, therefore Poles were guilty of what happened. The evidence for this kind of Jewish mythologization of the Holocaust, for understanding the meaning ascribed by Jews to Auschwitz, is not to be found in Poland today (the 'facts' are in any case far too elusive for that), but in the settled Jewish communities in the suburbs of London and New York, Paris and Tel Aviv. In a sense, the Jewish mystification of the Holocaust can be taken as the consequence of the concurrent belief in its uniqueness. Perhaps it is the refusal to consider that the Holocaust has a precedent, that there is indeed anything to compare it with, that represents the epistemological *sine qua non* of the mythologization of a catastrophe of such magnitude, despite its occurrence in recent history. But at least the mode of thinking is recognizable as a species of the mythological imagination: events and places are switched around, cause and effect are inverted, literality is abandoned, taboos emerge preventing ordinary discussion (for example, on the role of the Jews themselves in the Final Solution). The phenomenon is framed in a timelessness, whose inner workings are known only to specialists.

IV

What actually should be remembered about Auschwitz? What precisely? The interesting linguistic fact about the slogan 'Remember!' is that no direct object is supplied. The slogan is simply 'Remember!' In a sense the informants here are never so right as when they are wrong. For the mythological imagination it doesn't matter what precisely is to be remembered—the very fact that the slogan here supplies no direct object is another small piece of evidence that can be proposed for the mythologization of the event. The Jewish *vox populi* is in this sense ethnographically predictable with the use of this slogan, and in that sense, although the 19 empty plaques at Auschwitz–Birkenau are still waiting for their new inscription, Jews would probably feel that they can remain empty, silent, for a long time. For its part, the Ministry of Culture in Poland is entirely rational in its desire to see an agreed text for an inscription on this memorial as soon as possible. But reason and myth belong to two different discourses and trajectories. There is a sense in which the mythologization of Auschwitz does not depend at all on the text of the monument, that it hardly matters what inscription is finally erected there. Indeed, the very delay in finding a suitable inscription ironically mirrors the nature of the category which Auschwitz represents in the wider European folk imagination. After all, Jews— along with many other populations in Europe—probably feel that they do not need to visit Auschwitz and see the memorial there in order to confirm that the place exists in their own folk memory. Although the construction of a sacred text is an agonizing and agonized process, developed by many authors, the presumption has to be that the commentators and commentaries will in any case rush in at a later date to supply the meanings that are sought after and to spell them out for future generations who need the text being expounded. They could not do their job if the text did not have an aura of mystification about it; by definition, the text should not supply all the meanings. Best of all is if it remains ambiguous, semantically hanging in mid-air.

It may be, therefore, that the case of the inscription for the memorial at Auschwitz–Birkenau can push forward a little our understanding of memorial inscriptions generally. Uncertainty over the direct object nicely epitomizes the symbolic process at work. One is reminded of the image cited by G.K. Chesterton of the pilgrim who, having endured many hardships along the way to reach Jerusalem on foot, finally saw the Holy City surrounded by its beautiful walls and basking in the sunlight of an attractive spring morning. With that visual image before him, the pilgrim went no further: he turned around and went back where he had come from. He didn't want to sully his mythological picture of Jerusalem with the mundane secular realities of the place.[1] In many ways that image can help us in understanding what is happening in Auschwitz today. Those who sit on the International Auschwitz Council have been requested to supply the meanings of an Auschwitz which are not empirical but symbolic. Their attempt to construct a vernacular sacred text was agonizing. But the circumstances were exceptional: members of the Council included those who were themselves survivors of Auschwitz, as well as representatives of diverse interest groups. Under each other's watchful gaze, they had to attempt to construct an adequately reassuring mythological text that would remain symbolically meaningful for all those groups and yet more. Little wonder that Auschwitz, in the minds of some observers, can stand for little else than the world of an ultimate silence.

---

1.   G.K. Chesterton, *The New Jerusalem* (London: Hodder & Stoughton, n.d.), p. 77.

Part 2: Prayer

Introduction to Part 2: Prayer

Jon Davies and Isabel Wollaston

The words 'prayer' and 'precarious' share the same root; at times of doubt and danger people will fairly naturally address themselves to some powerful and, it is hoped, helpful force. The complex and timetabled rituals and sequences of ecclesiastical or authorized liturgies are a prime example of what Max Weber called the 'routinization' of the world; they address predicted problems, and once established they come to have an authority over and above their original purpose—and this is what they are meant to do, since one form of comfort does indeed lie in the insistence that nothing can happen which has not already happened; the 'comforting words' have already been spoken, the problems of the future have already been remembered.

In the three papers in this section, however, Burdi, Lovász and Lupo show how prayer is an enacted solicitation of help, depending for its subjective efficacy on the action of the praying person in 'personalizing' the prayer, as well as by the mobilization of more standard doxologies. All three papers make it clear that in day-to-day religious life there is no clear distinction between orthodoxy and 'heresy'; whether amongst the Nahua of Mexico or the Catholic peasants of southern Italy or eastern Hungary there is on offer both an official religion and a pre-Christian or pagan complement; and either may be invoked as and when required.

The three authors are linguists, although linguists with fieldwork experience, and there are clear echoes in their papers of the Frankfurt school of sociolinguistics, with its concern with the task of understanding 'everyday life'—an extraordinarily difficult cultural task. Official texts are very easily available, if only because official organizations make publicity and publication their business. 'Folk mores' or 'folk ways' are not so easily accessible; and praying—by far and away the most common doxology—has as much a private as a public occurrence. Lovász points out that the very act of trying to obtain information by asking questions can lead either to misunderstanding or to clamming up, because the act of asking questions in and of itself implies the end of the privacy of the prayer and praying person.

Burdi describes how the talismanic text which is called O'Retilio has a clandestine existence, being either burned or hidden in the walls of houses, because it is dangerous to own or to consult. Lupo describes how the Nahua Indians retain, within the formularies of orthodox Catholicism, a faithful rendition of an earlier, indigenous religion. All three authors, to repeat, stress that it is an act of praying itself which creates the possibility of synthesis: texts arise out of action. They may, therefore, disappear with the action—and depend for their translation into 'canon' on the temporary and largely accidental presence of a fieldworker!

It is tempting to think that the great authorized or official theologies of the modern world, with their huge emphasis on the written form as the expression of orthodoxy, emerged out of oral cultures, such as those described by Burdi, Lupo and Lovász. The Venerable Bede, himself writing many years after the events he describes, depicts the encounter between the literate world of the Roman Catholic missionary Augustine and the oral culture of the pagans he encountered in the southern parts of Britain; and much of the story of the expansion of Christianity in Europe is of a written text achieving canonical status simply because it was written. The pagan oral tradition cannot be canonized, and perhaps survived because of that, whether in Mexico or Britain or Hungary, where it persists as myth and inchoate icon, as fable and folklore, addressing itself to the written words of orthodoxy all the more readily because the act of praying is by definition an oral practice. Just as the invention and ownership of spurs put a premium on horse-borne soldiery, and thereby gave military dominance to those rich enough to own warhorses, so the control of the expensive business of writing must have given superordinate canonical status to the favoured documents of those larger ecclesiastical establishments which could afford scriptoria and scribes. A culture that is written down is for that reason capable of being policed: it may then be canonized—or anathematized. Oral cultures are much more difficult to police: they can be degraded, harassed, ridiculed, but never effectively repressed, as they return always to challenge the established canon, which is itself precarious precisely because its primal vigour derived from the same source as its challenger.

Prayer, then, is an act on the boundary between the canonized and the anathematized, a permanent source of challenge and creativity, of obedience and resistance. The utterance of a prayer is an act of evaluation of the liturgy, giving the praying person the ability to have both the comfort of the Word and the satisfaction of his or her own words. All texts, when canonized, become less than enough: a sacred text is a selection of texts, a selection of prayers, a limitation of supplicatory options. The sacred words of the world are limitless, human need of them endless: sacred texts are limited editions. Heresy in prayer is therefore normal.

It is necessary to note that Hungary and Italy, the areas of fieldwork of Lovász and Burdi, have been areas of Christian missionary activity and Christian dominance for many centuries, while Mexico has seen the deployment of the same religion for nearly five hundred years. Even Mexico's 'vernacular' must include, by now, a rather deeply rooted Christian iconography and language. The best-remembered icons are not necessarily those with the *longest* pedigree, but those most closely identified with the most *potent* pedigree. It is also the case, we would suggest, that as present concerns and social conditions vary, so will the nature of what is remembered vary: as Freud insisted, the past is an act of deliberate choice, a contrived calculus of remembering and forgetting. All of our first-year students could remember Barabbas (two thousand years dead) but none of them could remember Hereward the Wake (one thousand years dead)—and this included a boy whose first name was Hereward! Christianity is, to repeat, the vernacular religion as well as the official religion of Europe and European culture; and all religious acts, from the most public to the most private, will mobilize a Christian view of God: this does not, as our three fieldworkers show, mean that they will mobilize only the official view of God.

The Powerful and Perilous Text: The Symbolism of the 'Book' in a Southern Italian Village

Patrizia Burdi

While fieldwork is aimed at acquiring knowledge of specific topics, the conversational nature of one's approach often keeps the informer from restricting his or her response to the areas formulated. The result is information and reports ranging far outside the scope of the original question, extraneous details often jotted down by the anthropologist out of mere professional duty.

A rereading of such 'eclectic' data does, however, reap precious fruits. On the one hand, it allows for observation of the explicative and associative processes set in motion by the actor on the social scene. On the other hand, it may shed some light on the existence of connections and superimpositions that the investigator's attentive and rational eye tends to dismiss as impossible and therefore unworthy of scientific attention.

This is true of the data that inspired this paper, data collected in an interior region of the southern Italian Appennines—Sannio in the Benevento district (more specifically, in the village of San Marco dei Cavoti)—during a study of ethnomedicine.[1] In this isolated area of southern Italy, as in many of the country's non-urbanized regions, there is still a well-defined, fairly viable corpus of traditional knowledge which organizes the concepts and conduct of medicine and healing. Here the level of ability is determined by the type of knowledge and the means by which this knowledge is acquired.[2]

---

1.   This data was collected under the direction of Professor Signorini of La Sapienza University, Rome, and was funded by this University.

2.   See P. Burdi, 'Spiriti, Santi e "Buonsenso": Ideologia e Prassi di Alcuni Guaritori in una Valle del'Alto Sannio', *L'Uomo* 1.1-2 (1988), pp. 191-219; and *idem*, 'Il Sapere ed il Potere Terapeutico: Guaritori, Maghi e Pazienti in un Contesto Rurale dell'Italia Meridionale' (PhD dissertation, La Sapienza University, Rome,

Whether these widely different forms of healing involve manipulation, exorcism or simply rogation, there is always a constant in the recital of verbal formulae: this is 'the conceptual fulcrum and is, of all ritual actions, the one which amalgamates the capacity of fascination and symbolic meaning to the greatest degree'.[1] It is widely known that the study of medicine within traditional and/or exotic contexts requires entering into the complex universe of magic, and establishing which instruments and powers are used to heal or harm. The vast majority of the formulae within the set of prayers, enchantments, invocations or injunctions used can be traced primarily to Catholic verbal liturgy, albeit with traditional elaboration. There is, however, a constant reference to the formulae that call up supernatural forces of an evil nature or that can magically manipulate reality. The formulae referring to the divine are part of collective knowledge and are the object of exchange and communication, appearing as a blessing, a value to be preserved.

The magically oriented formulae constitute the essence of esoteric knowledge and represent an individual and therefore dangerous possession whose power lies in the secrecy with which it is safeguarded. Access to this esoteric knowledge involves either an apprenticeship with a *maano* (the local term for sorcerer)[2] or the possession of texts on magic which vary immensely. There is, in fact, a flourishing, if underground, circulation of booklets known as 'treatises on magic'. They are genuine popular pamphlets crammed with formulae, invocations and instructions on how to become a perfect sorcerer, and can be purchased from any railway news-stand. But in depressed areas like the one under study, their possession and, more importantly, the ability to read them, is still an element denoting the use of, or at least the intention to possess, evil powers. They place the individual possessing them in a treacherous position in relation to the community.

This paper will deal with a text regarded as both magical and sacred, the vision that the local population has of it in contrast to its

1991).

1.   Burdi, 'Il Sapere ed il Potere Terapeutico', p. 128.

2.   The same term also implies the function of witches: they are, for example, the only male exponents traditionally supposed to take part in the infernal sabbat at the 'Noce di Benevento'.

actual content (consulted in the National Library, Rome), and with a myth bizarrely connected to it.

During interviews on approaches to learning healing, one book was often cited. According to our informants, it was the primary magic text. There were times when the description of the book and the circumstances and eventualities connected with its possession was followed by an account of certain actions by a certain character, with no apparent connection between the two apart from the name: Rutilio.

For the moment we will disregard other characters with the same name who nevertheless do slip into the subject under examination. We can state, however, that Rutilio is also the Christian name of the author of a book which really does exist, *Almanacco Perpetuo* (Perpetual Almanac), by Benincasa (1555–c.1626), first published in 1601. The thirtieth edition appeared in 1732, and the last edition we know of appeared in 1915. The edition we employed was published in the second half of the seventeenth century, possibly in 1684. This almanac, an exemplary compendium of Renaissance knowledge, is divided into five parts, each of which is composed of tractates subdivided into chapters. The first two parts are of the greatest interest. The first deals with astrology, and includes an analysis of the planets, describing their characteristics and astral paths (Tractates I and II), along with predictions about agriculture and the climate. Subsequent tractates deal with politics (Tractate III), tables for calculation of the mobile holidays, the Golden Number, the Epact and other curiosities, and the classification of time (Tractate IV), the influence of the planets on nature and humanity, and the interpretation of human physiognomy (Tractate V), the size of the celestial orbs and the lifetime of the planet (Tractate VI), and 'the most notable things which have happened in the world, beginning with its creation' (Tractate VII). This first part provides a masterly illustration of the value that an astrological approach attaches to time, likened to destiny, and conceived of as a primordial principle. This importance is illustrated by the fanatical attention given to the calculation of every part of its length and their deification.[1] By contrast, the second part concentrates on rules for good health (Tractate I), ideas about anatomy and, once again, the influence of the signs of the Zodiac on parts of the human body (Tractate II). The last three parts were later additions by Ottavio

1.   F. Cumont, *Le Religioni Orientali nel Paganesimo Romano* (Bara: Laterza, 1967), pp. 191-224.

Beltrano, another scholar from southern Italy. They deal primarily with matters of agriculture, navigation, arithmetic, geometry and the art of war.

We now turn to the indigenous vision of the text. *O'Retilio*, as the locals call it,[1] is considered to be the quintessence of human and non-human knowledge: 'Retilio knew all there was, things of the future and things bygone, more than even God above'. The book's potential for predicting the future and its presumed omniscience, even greater than that of the Creator, immediately identifies it as an instrument of the Evil One, and even, as we shall see later on, as his materialization. It is, in fact, a book written *malamente* (an adverb referring to all that is demonic and magical), even though numerous informants insisted that not all its parts are regarded in this light. Pages copied by hand and considered 'innocuous' deal with good and bad days for falling sick (Second Part, Tractate I, Chapter X) and taking blood (Second Part, Tractate II, Chapter VIII). Furthermore, popular beliefs still contain ideas concerning the farming cycle and meteorological phenomena that are found in the original text.[2]

The book's negative aspects are further underscored by the fact that it brought trouble and misfortune upon whoever possessed it: 'whoever possessed it was soon destroyed, and, if he lived, became the most wretched being of all'. In the past, it was common practice to burn copies in circulation or to hide them, generally within the walls of houses. However, the most striking element which singles out copies of the book as an emanation of the Evil One was the ability of anyone who consulted it to command the service of supernatural forces. According to our informants, the reader of the book hears a voice offering to obey his other commands, somewhat like the genie in Aladdin's lamp: 'When you attain a command, you hear a veritable voice—'Command me, Father'—and should the command be unknown, the troubles, they come in droves'.

Responses to specific questions on the text's nature and use were

1.   For its diffusion in the Sannio area, see A. De Spirito, *Il Paese delle Streghe: Una Ricerca Sulla Magia nel Sannio Campano* (Rome: Bulzoni, 1976), pp. 109-16.

2.   For example, the area's still common belief regarding the influence of winds on conception which the book's author cites as an 'opinion of Aristotle' (Part 1, Tractate VII, Chapter XXII): the woman whose union takes place when the north wind blows will give birth to a son while, if the southerly or south-easterly winds blow, she will give birth to a daughter.

often phrased as accounts of episodes where the main character is a foolish reader who, unable to 'command', either finds himself terrified by the appearance of supernatural phenomena (such as spiders, lizards or beetles between the pages of the book, or of sudden hail storms), or becomes the victim of actual violence.

A careful analysis of the original text shows that none of its pages contains any reference to ceremonial magic or the evocation of supernatural powers. We may therefore conclude that it is the text itself, and particularly the sections on astrology, that lead to its being viewed as an instrument of magical coercion, if not a manifestation of supernatural forces. Dominant Catholic opinion regards the latter as evil by definition. Finally, the ability to read the book without any unpleasant consequences is considered proof of knowledge, and thus of power. In the traditional context under consideration, power is not identified with action, but rather with wisdom—primarily with the ability to read, the fundamental source of knowledge, and, as such, a source of prestige and authority, however ambiguous.

Ethnographic data became more complex and difficult to interpret when the straightforward accounts of strange events accompanying the reading of the book were juxtaposed with seemingly unrelated versions of a myth concerning the aforementioned Rutilio. As well as having the same name as both the book and its author, he is likened to it: Rutilio is both the book and an individual. My research uncovered two versions of this 'myth'. The first and more straightforward version goes as follows. Rutilio was a man who existed with God before Christ. In order to be reborn, he cut himself into pieces and placed himself in a bottle, burying himself in a dung heap to keep warm. A pig dug up the bottle, a fact which interrupted Rutilio's period of gestation after only seven months. As a result, neither Rutilio nor any other human being could ever attain immortality: 'God did not let him out because He knew that, were the creature to be born again, He would lose command of the world. If the creature were to be reborn, we could never again be born and the world would then be always and only him'.

The second version of the myth is more elaborate: the story is set just prior to the appearance of Jesus in the world. There was widespread anticipation of the coming of a king who would be master of the earth and sky in opposition to the Devil. Rutilio, the master of the earth, realized that the coming of the messiah would destroy his own power. He therefore ordered his sister to kill him and cut him up into tiny pieces ('she was to cut a piece from every joint'). She was to put the pieces into a bottle, cork it, and bury it in a dung heap, so that the heat would help the process of gestation and the being would be born after nine months. However, God decreed that his Son should be born beforehand, for if Jesus were to be born afterwards, he would have no influence in the world ('He would be no one'). The police of the time ('the law') accused Rutilio's sister of making him disappear. In her own defence, she pointed out that she was only acting in accordance with her brother's wishes. To conclude: Rutilio's sister was forced to bring him to the surface before he could be completely reformed, and he was born with horns in the seventh month.

Although some of the key elements of this strange tale—notably the being's mutilation and rebirth, and the crucial presence of a character, the sister—have been reworked in the light of Catholicism, it is reminiscent of the myth of Osiris, widespread in the world of the Mediterranean and the Near East. While the Pyramid Texts (2500–2270 BCE) do not provide a coherent and detailed version of the myth, the main lines do not differ greatly from its presentation by Plutarch.[1] Osiris was an ancient king who was killed and cut into pieces by his jealous brother, Seth. The pieces of his body were sought for and gathered up by Isis, his sister–consort. Osiris was resurrected and, with Isis, begot a son, Horus, who avenged his father and became lord of the dead.

Before offering a comparison of these two myths, I would like to point out that the origins of such a comparison lie not so much in the unlikely conjunction of elements drawn from two totally different cultural and historical contexts. They are to be found, rather, in the documented existence of Egyptian cults in the region under investigation. According to Cumont, there is proof that such cults were already widespread in the South of Italy as early as the last century BCE. They were to be found in the Latin world until the end of the fourth century CE.[2] From the second century CE, such cults were to be found

1. See J.G. Griffiths, *Plutarch's De Iside et Osiride* (Cardiff: University of Wales Press, 1970) and *The Origins of Osiris and his Cult* (Leiden: Brill, 1980). See also Frazer's treatment of this myth in J.G. Frazer, *The Golden Bough* (London: Macmillan, 1914).

2. Cumont, *Le Religioni Orientali nel Paganesimo Romano*, pp. 101-29. Among the various works dealing with the development of Eastern cults in Italy, see

throughout the region of Campania, from Pozzuoli, the largest port in the Italian sea.[1] Characteristically, they developed not through official, institutional religious channels, but as expressions of popular devotion, fed by the vast array of merchants, soldiers, slaves and bondsmen who landed on the peninsula's southern coast, particularly from Delos and Sicily.[2] These new arrivals brought with them practices and beliefs connected with Alexandrian divinities.

The ease with which these Egyptian religious elements were assimilated was due, first of all, to their flexibility and adaptability in contexts very different from their original environment.[3] Here, there was a constant process of syncretism, whereby the major divinities absorbed the characteristics of local gods. The assimilation of Isis with a number of divinities in the Graeco-Roman world (for example Demeter, Aphrodite and Hera) bears witness to this process. Furthermore, it should be noted that from an archaeological perspective Benevento is the most important site for original Egyptian sculptures in the West, and confirms 'the existence of an Isis cult of primary importance'.[4] The presence of proof of the vitality of Egyptian cults in southern Italy, particularly in Benevento, can shed light on the way in which the Rutilio myth is interpreted. Before beginning our analysis, a further connection with the Osiris myth should also be noted. Alongside reference to Domitian in hieroglyphic

J. Leclant, 'Notes sur la propagation des cultes et monuments Egyptiens en Occident, a l'époque impériale', *Bulletin de l'Institut Francais d'Archéologie Orientale* 55 (1956), pp. 173-79; V. Tran Tam Tinh, *Essai sur le culte de Isis à Pompéi* (Paris: de Boccard, 1964); R.E. Witt, *Isis in the Graeco-Roman World* (London: Thames & Hudson, 1971); M. Malaise, *Inventaire préliminaire des documents égyptiens découverts en Italie* (Leiden: Brill, 1972).

1.   See H.W. Muller, *Il Culto di Iside nell'antica Benevento* (Benevento: Saggi e Studi del Museo del Sannio, 1971), p. 19.

2.   See M. Malaise, *Les conditions de pénétration et de diffusion des cultes égyptiens en Italie* (Leiden: Brill, 1972).

3.   According to Cumont, 'the nebulous ideas of Eastern priests allow each to perceive his own phantoms therein. . . The gods are all and they are nothing, they are lost and have vanished' (*Le Religioni Orientali nel Paganesimo Romano*, p. 115; my translation).

4.   Muller, *Il Culto di Iside nell'antica Benevento*, p. 13. The inscriptions on the obelisks found in the city refer to Isis as the 'lady of Benevento' (p. 25), while the cult of Osiris can be spied in the canopic vase, the vase containing holy water, considered to be an emanation of the Divinity (p. 26). See also Malaise, *Les conditions de pénétration et de diffusion des cultes égyptiens en Italie*, pp. 204-207.

inscriptions on two obelisks in Benevento, we also find the name of the Roman officer responsible for their erection, and who held a position of some importance in the city: Rutilius Lupus.[1]

To return to our original story and its connection with the myth of Osiris, it immediately becomes apparent that the later Catholic reworking of the story results in the comparison of the main character with Christ. Of the three structural elements common to both narratives (divine royalty, dismemberment, and a woman's redemptive function), the last of these has been altered. Rutilio, like Christ, is a king whose empire encompasses the whole world,[2] but the only way he can attain immortality, and thereby defeat death, is by the decomposition of his body. Unlike Osiris, Rutilio is unsuccessful because of the involvement of his sister (Isis's involvement, by contrast, results in the resurrection of Osiris). In the Catholic reading, Rutilio's mutilation and death cannot be followed by an resurrection worthy of the name because this would thwart the arrival on earth of the real God, Christ. The actions of Rutilio's sister therefore enable the real holder of immortality to acquire the title which was bestowed upon Osiris: 'the first who rose from the dead'.[3] In contrast to Christ, the false god has horns, the indelible mark of evil.

To conclude: if the fate of Osiris is the pagan model of resurrection, it is plausible to assume that this model might remain in the popular imagination, particularly in an area where the cult predominated. It is also likely that this model would be altered to conform with Christian teaching, and condemned as an abortive attempt

---

1.   Curiously enough, he has the same name as an Egyptian prefect under Trajan in the year 113 CE, who seems to belong to 'the ancient house of the Rutilii Lupi, apparently from Benevento' (A. Stein, *Die Präfekten von Ägypten in der Römischen Kaiserzeit* [Berne: A. Francke, 1950], p. 58; my translation). The Latin author who observed and described a celebration of Osiris (*Renovatus Osiris*) in Faleria, a town on the banks of a tributary of the Tiber, was also named Rutilius (Namantianus). In that celebration the resurrection of the divinity was connected to the cycle of agricultural renewal.

2.   We might add another common element of an instrumental nature, i.e. the dismembered body's container: the bottle in which Rutilio's limbs were placed recalls the vase which ritually represented the object of the Osiris cult in Benevento.

3.   Apropos of this, Wallis Budge states that, 'both Plutarch and Diodorus agree in assigning a divine origin to Osiris, and both state that he reigned in the form of a man upon the earth' (Osiris and the Egyptian Resurrection [London: Warren, 1911], pp. 6, 28).

in comparison to the Catholic model. Thus, it would appear that the connection between the tale of Rutilio (which we might see as a popular Catholic version of the Osiris myth) and the book (which is both desired and feared) lies in the name. It is the name which serves to link all these seemingly diverse elements. On the one hand, we have a text regarded as sacred and a superimposed mythical figure. On the other hand, there are two historical characters (the Roman officer and the author of *Almanaco Perpetuo*) connected with ancient Egyptian culture, albeit for entirely different reasons: the former through the Roman appropriation of local cults in order to increase its hold on the empire, the latter through the use of astrology, the art of the temples of Chaldea and Egypt.

The magical power of the name, the mystical coincidence between the designation and the individual to which it refers, would appear to supply an interpretive key to the collected data, and it also emerges as an important element in the popular tradition of Benevento, just as it was for adherents of the Osiris cult, whether in Egypt or the Roman Empire. In the daily liturgy dedicated to the Alexandrian gods, the opening of the sanctuary, the libations and ceremonial hymns were followed by the calling of the gods by name. Only at this point did the gods awaken from their sleep, ready to obey those who called them.[1] As Cassirer notes, 'as the sphere of a being's power increases, and as mythical significance accumulates, the significance of its name becomes greater'.[2] What is true for the name, expression and verbal determination of thought, is even more applicable to the written word (of which the book is the concrete manifestation). In the context outlined in this paper, the book is primarily of value in itself, and only secondarily in relation to its contents. In this instance, the sacredness of the text arises from its ritual use, and from the association with supernatural forces. Last but not least, sacredness is found in the associated myth, which emphasizes the negative value of those forces.

Aside from historical and social explanations of the virtual absence of books from the rural landscape, a book emerges as both a form and instrument of power. It gives method and shape to the collective imagination to generate seemingly irrational connections and superimpositions, thus nurturing symbolic and evocative power.

1. See Cumont, *Le Religioni Orientali nel Paganesimo Romano*, p. 123.
2. E. Cassirer, *Linguaggio e Mito* (Milan: Il Saggiatore, 1961), p. 83; my translation.

Oral Christianity in Hungary: Interpreting Interpretations

Irén Lovász

Introduction

As Peter Berger states, 'Religion is a humanly constructed universe of meaning, and this construction is undertaken by linguistic means'.[1] Therefore, if we accept that religion appears in texts and sets examples in texts, and I use the word text in its widest meaning to include written, verbal, visual and ritual texts, then these two trends are strongly related to the two main functions of religion we define as 'model for' and 'model of' functions in cultural anthropology, based on C. Geertz's idea.[2] According to this thesis religion, on the one hand, is a model *for* reality. From this point of view a sacred text serves as a model for people's behaviour in the creation of their everyday life world and in the formation of their own personal reality. On the other hand it is also a model *of* reality. Sacred texts give meaning to as well as interpret social and psychological reality with the help of conceptual forms. My topic deals with a genre of religious oral tradition. I would like to show how the 'model of' and 'model for' aspects of religion are present in prayers.

Archaic folk prayer is one of the most ancient forms, and at the same time one of the most recently discovered genres, of Hungarian folklore. It was not officially accepted by the Hungarian Academy of Sciences until 1970, when the discoverer of the genre, Zsuzsanna Erdeelyi,[3] presented and described it. She distinguished the

1. P. Berger, *The Sacred Canopy* (Garden City, NY: Doubleday, 1967), p. 175.
2. C. Geertz, 'Religion as a Cultural System', in Michael Banton (ed.), *Anthropological Approaches to the Study of Religion* (London: Tavistock, 1966), p. 7.
3. Zs. Erdeelyi, *Hegyet Hagek, Lotot Lepek* (Archaic Folk Prayers) (Budapest: Magrebo Publishers, 1976).

following main types of prayers according to motifs and contents:

1. Incantation and defensive formula: this type mixes pagan and Christian world concepts.
2. Texts with purely Christian motivation and conceptualization, and the interpretation of biblical stories (for example the dialogue between Christ and Mary, Mary's search for Christ, Mary's mourning of Christ, Pilate and Golgotha, Mary's dream, and so on).
3. Texts in connection with medieval church literature.
4. Privately inspired texts.
5. Texts with a melody to be sung as prayers, Christmas and New Years' songs.[1]

I wish to define these prayers as *verbal* means of sacred communication. Since both the texts and their performance were considered illicit by the church for centuries, they had to be practised in secret and have therefore preserved ancient features of the language and world concept of the early Hungarians. Both 'sacred' and 'secret' imply special linguistic forms, special acts of speech, and special pragmatic conditions. These texts were the means of secret, hidden, underground, illegal communication with the Sacred. The basis of this tradition is a desire for extra devotion. This kind of praying is usually done at home in private and does not belong to the liturgical actions of the church. Most of the texts we are familiar with are used by both Roman and Greek Catholics in Hungary, but we can also find a few in Protestant tradition.

The speciality of this genre is the *concluding formula*, which confirms the authorization and divine certification of the utilization and effectiveness of these texts. The words are as follows:

> Our Lord Jesus Christ himself said:
> Sacred word, Sacred speech:
> whoever says this prayer
> morning and evening
> wins the Kingdom of Heaven.
> or: his seven deadly sins will be forgiven.
> or: he wins sixty days indulgence.

1. Erdeelyi, *Hegyet Hagek.*

Thus the prayer is valid only for the person who says it in this form, or so it is believed. The combination of the sacred and secret factor could be regarded as a guarantee for the conservation of religious texts in several cultures.[1]

Understanding, Interpreting

Gadamer argued that, 'hermeneutics was originally connected with the sphere of sacredness in which an authoritative will is expressed towards those it addresses... and the hidden original normative meaning can be found during the course of theological and philological interpretations of these classic and sacred texts and the juristic interpretation of laws'.[2] In the case of these prayers, as the concluding formula indicates, an authoritative will is being followed. God's will is expressed in the text and in this way works as a model for people's behaviour. This is the reason why these prayers still exist and are still practised. It is also the reason why the church banned these texts and forbade their practice for centuries. The development of the religious field, in the sense of Bourdieau,[3] goes hand in hand with the fact that the chosen body of priests monopolizes everything which offers salvation. It monopolizes by (re)producing the consciously organized group of secret religious knowledge. The development of the religious field, therefore, goes hand in hand with the objective exclusion of those who become profane through this very process. Religious capital accumulates in the hands of a small group while the excluded are robbed of this capital. This leads to the symbolic division of 'sacred knowledge' and 'profane ignorance'. This division is expressed and strengthened by various secrets on the different sides. The essence of the contrast between the sacred and the profane, and the contrast between the legitimate usage of sacraments (religion) and the profane usage of sacraments (magic or witchcraft) is identical to the contrast between the monopolizers of the handling of sacred things and the

---

1.   I. Lovász, 'Szent Szo, Szent Berzed' ('Sacred Language, Sacred Speech'), in M. Hoppal and E. Pentikainen (eds.), *Northern Religions and Shamanism* (n.p.; n.d.).

2.   H.G. Gadamer, 'Hermeneutics', in E. Csikos and L. Lakatos (eds.), *Hermeneutic Philosophy* (Budapest, 1990).

3.   P. Bourdieau, *The Genesis and Structure of the Study of Religion* (Budapest: Gondoki, 1978), 13.12.

uninitiated.[1] In the case of the prayers at issue the conflict is caused by the obtaining of forgiveness and indulgence in ways not recognized in the regulations. The church labelled forgiveness and indulgence obtained without its intervention illegitimate, for this was the privilege of the Pope alone from the thirteenth century. These prayers were deemed 'theologice liturgice absurdum' by Hungarian priests even in the 1970s. This reaction of the church was completely natural, for 'any practice or belief that is oppressed inevitably appears profane in that it questions the monopoly of handling sacred things by its mere existence, and thus the legitimacy of the proprietor of this monopoly. This is why the survival of old beliefs is at the same time a form of resistance. It expresses the fact that the faithful will not allow themselves to be robbed of the tools of religious production'.[2] Whoever prays this prayer questions the legality of the monopolization of religious possessions by making direct contact between the profane individual and the sacred. On top of it all, divine powers validate his or her actions. ('Our Lord Christ himself said... whoever says this prayer... his seven deadly sins will be forgiven'.)

The prayers were handed down over centuries from parent to child, grandparent to grandchild. They never really left the house. Not even relatives or neighbours knew of each others' prayers. The fact that our archives have a collection of tens of thousands of them is the benefit of a bishop's letter of 1972 (thanks to the good intentions of a single bishop) stressing the historiocultural value of the texts, deeming them theologically harmless, piously supportable, and encouraging priests and believers alike to bring them out into the open in the interest of science. During the course of my most recent fieldwork (24 May 1991) the parson of Gyimesfelsolok said to me, 'It doesn't matter that the people say these superstitious prayers. They can't help it; they are theologically ignorant. What counts is that these prayers help keep the feeling of remorse alive. They come to church to confess anyway.'

These texts have little in common with official 'priestly' prayers but they are related to historical ecclesiastical literature, especially to medieval religious poetry, the main goal of which is the depiction and the direct experience of Christ the Saviour's death and Mary's motherly pain. The central theme of the prayers is the *story of suffering*. Two characteristics of medieval religious practice can be found in the

1. Bourdieau, *Genesis and Structure*, p. 182.
2. Bourdieau, *Genesis and Structure*, p. 184.

background of this compassion (the wish to suffer and die together): the rosary and the *via crucis*. The *via crucis* was made popular in Hungary by Franciscan practice as part of the concept of Imitatio Christi.

While reciting these prayers the person praying experiences Christ's life and death or Mary's pain just the same as when walking the Stations of the Cross. The Way of the Cross, the Calvary, helps people experience the sacred event of the past and makes it more personal through repetition. These texts do the same thing: by reciting them the scene from the Bible is ritually repeated, personally experienced, recalled and validated to the one who recites them. During the course of experiencing the story the people praying often begin to cry. Women praying experience Mary's pain as if it were their own.

Autocommunication

In this case the texts operate in an autocommunicative way similar to Jurij Lotman's example:[1] a woman reading *Anna Karenina* may simply regard the book as yet more information on the Russian railway system, or on society and human destiny; or she can say 'I am Anna'—and she thereby not only alters and broadens the book but also reconsiders and re-evaluates herself, her relationships and her actions. She imposes Anna Karenina's fate upon herself: the novel's text has worked in an autocommunicative way. According to Lotman[2] two modes of communication can be defined which differentiate between cultural groups. The first mode is the traditional sender–receiver format (I–Him); it quantitively adds to the receiver's knowledge. The second mode is autocommunication (I–I), communication addressed to oneself. Autocommunication is typical of artistic and religious texts, but any text can be autocommunicational. An autocommunicational text (novel, poem, prayer, mantra) can be read many times over. Its function, however, is not to add information in the quantitative sense but to qualitatively enhance the ego or team spirit of a group. This type of text functions as a code rather than a message or information, transforming the identity and self-image of the reader. Then, using

1.   J. Lotman, 'Odruh modelah kommunikacii' (On Models of Communication within Culture'), in *Trudy po znakovym sistermam*, 6 (1975), p. 238.
2.   Lotman, 'Odruh modelah kommunikacii'.

any text as a code, we say to ourselves, 'this touches me, this is meant for me'.

In the case of our prayers people reciting them say, 'this is my life. This could be my life. I imitate Christ's life (Imitatio Christi). I experience Mary's motherly pain,' and so on. At the same time the reciter reflects her own personal pain on to Mary (for example if a woman loses her son).

Any text can have an everyday meaning and an autocommunicative interpretation. Very often both are present. The first transmits surplus information while the second materializes through emotive codes and touches the reader.

This opposition corresponds to what Roland Barthes writes about the two types of photography. One is the *studium*, the other the *punctum*, type of photograph.[1] The first informs while the other 'touches the heart with point-like sharpness. It moves the viewer'. The punctum type triggers shock-like enlightenment in the viewer (as in the reader) whom Barthes calls the spectator. He describes this moment with the Japanese Buddhist expression 'Satori'.[2] The prototype of Barthes' studium–punctum opposition can be found in his earlier works in which he attempts to understand the meaning of film (*Le troisieme sense*, 1970), and literary texts and the phenomenology of reading (*Le plaisir du text*, 1973).[3]

All the traits Lotman describes as unique to texts functioning as a code rather than as information are characteristic of archaic folk prayers. They are rythmic series, repetitions and complementary systems, and are totally immaterial to the I–Him type of communication system.[4]

A national culture as well as an individual can perform a reading with a second code by saying, 'This text represents our culture, it is us'.[5] Autocommunication is the main channel of myths. 'Every organization has an autocommunicative, myth-producing, autoportrative

1. R. Barthes, *Camera Lucida: Reflections on Photography* (Chaucer Press, 1982).

2. Barthes, *Camera Lucida*, p. 109.

3. I. Lovász, 'Barthes', *Janus* 1.4 (1986).

4. Lovász, 'Sacred Language, Sacred Speech'.

5. H. Broms and H. Gahmberg, *The Semiotics of Management* (Helsinki, 1987).

element'.[1] I share Leach's idea that in the case of ritual performances 'there is no separate audience of listeners. The performers and the listeners are the same people. We engage in rituals in order to transmit collective messages to ourselves'.[2] Rites, just like myths, tell us something about ourselves to ourselves.

At this point we have arrived at the problem of myth and reality, or text and truth. In my opinion the basis of thinking about myths is to accept that a myth is a reality for those who read, use and believe in it. A text is reality itself, and the word and the thing are the same.[3] This, I think, is the fundamental basis of sacred language and sacred texts. It implies that a word will come true, that the utterance of a word is an act which creates reality. This is my point of departure in the interpretation of archaic folk prayers.

Folklore Facts and Speech Acts

In my opinion prayers can be interpreted as actions, not only as texts, for they are not merely texts but rituals of saying and reciting. They exist in utterance, in performance. They are kept alive by the ancient belief that the spoken word has creative and active power, that the Word will come true. Other archaic forms of speech were founded on the belief in magic and the creative power of the word, for example blessings, curses and incantations. Since by saying the text as part of the performance, the performative action, we are in fact executing the action of blessing, cursing, incanting and praying, I consider these manifestations as speech acts.

The application of speech-act theory comes naturally in this case, since the origin of the theory is that there are words and sentences which, when said, perform certain actions rather than just stating facts; that is, we display performative manifestations as well as constative ones.[4] Unlike constative manifestations, performative ones cannot be true or false, only successful or unsuccessful.

Types of illocutionary (performative) acts as defined by John

1.   H. Broms, *The Semiotics of Culture* (Helsinki, 1988).
2.   E. Leach, *Culture and Communication* (Cambridge: Cambridge University Press, 1976).
3.   See E. Cassirer, *Essay on Man* (New Haven, 1944).
4.   See J.L. Austin, *How to do Things with Words* (Budapest: Akademia, 1990).

Searle[1] are the following: (1) to request, (2) to assert, state (that), affirm, (3) to question, (4) to thank (for), (5) to advise, (6) to warn, (7) to greet, (8) to congratulate. Prayer, curse, blessing and incantation formulae seem to belong to the first category of illocutionary acts, the request category, since they meet all the requirements and rules which must be met in order for this speech act to be successful, as follows:

Propositional Content:	A future act (A) is sought from H.
Preparatory:	1. He is able to do A. S believes H is able to do A.
	2. It is not obvious to S and H that H will do A at his own accord
Sincerity:	S wants H to do A.
Essential:	Counts as an attempt to get H to do A.
Comment:	Order and command have the additional preparatory rule that S must be in a position of *authority* over H. Command probably does not have the 'pragmatic' condition requiring non-obviousness. Furthermore, the authoritative relationship in both affects the essential condition, since the verbalization counts as an attempt to get H to do A in virtue of the authority of S over H.

It is obvious that in the case of incantation the request is formed as a command or order. Because the reciter possesses the text, he or she believes himself or herself superior to the illness or demon and is therefore able to order them to do something directly. The request in the case of the *prayer* in this aspect is exactly the opposite: pleading and begging are the typical form. The reciter turns to the Heavenly Power he or she considers his or her respected superior, and asks for the accomplishment of A. He or she humbly asks H to do A.

The request is placed indirectly in the case of a *blessing* or *curse*. The reciter only refers to the Heavenly Power. Certain types and parts of the prayers can also belong to Searle's second and fourth categories, not only the first: thanksgiving, gratitude, declaration, statement, affirmation.[2] I cannot elaborate on silent prayers at this point and on other forms of non-verbal manifestations, or on the typical pragmatic function of prayers, the offer, which Searle does not mention among his categories.

---

1.   J. Searle, *Speech Acts: An Essay in the Philosophy of Language* (Cambridge: Cambridge University Press, 1969).
2.   See my comments in 'Szent Szo, Szent Berzed', pp. 334-35.

I have examined how these pragmatic conditions and standards pertain to archaic folk prayers. First I looked for linguistic signs that can be felt directly: the *vocative* and the *imperative*. The vocative is the most typical form of prayer in general, in which the reciter addresses the Heavenly Power: S turns to H directly. I found a very few examples of this: my Lord, my Creator, my dear Heavenly Saint Father, oh my Sweet Jesus, my Provident Father, oh beautiful Blessed Mother Mary, Hail Star of the Sea, Mary, Star of the Sky, His Majesty the Lord God, oh Lord Jesus Christ. In cases where an address (vocative) is the introductory formula there is always a request (imperative): free me, give, don't allow, take away, beseech, cleanse, let us not stray, let us enter, let us see, let us follow, let them come, and so on.

According to my observations these texts never have the typical prayer concluding formula ('Christ our Lord said, whoever says this prayer...'). It is also worthy of mention that these texts belong to the third and fourth categories of prayers and are therefore listed among texts related to medieval church literature and other miscellaneous texts.[1]

I have concluded my observations in the other direction as well. According to these results those prayers which do have a concluding formula do not have a vocative (the addressing of God) and do not have a request formula (imperative). These texts do not therefore include the pragmatic functions (the request or plea directed towards the addressed power) typical of 'classic' prayers.

Taking these traits into account we can clearly define a category of prayers which ends in a specific formula and does not include either an address or a request, the category of archaic folk prayers. (The only exception to this is in the case of contaminated, syncretic texts.) The question is why 'pure' archaic folk prayers do not include a request or address as 'classic' prayers do. Why does the person praying not enact the request or plea by reciting the prayer? It is because there is no need for it: these texts are 'useful', 'effective' and 'strong' prayers just the way they are. These are the terms their reciters use. Proof of their effectiveness is comprised in the clause, 'Our Lord Christ himself said: Sacred word, sacred speech, whoever says this prayer, his seven deadly sins will be forgiven'.

The clause as part of the text is about the text. It is on a level high

1.   See Erdeelyi, *Hegyet Hagek*.

above the text, the level of metacommunication. It tells us how to interpret the text. It is the 'key' of Del Hymes.[1] One of my sources even added, 'This is no joke. Christ our Lord said this himself'. As the text states, this is 'sacred word, sacred speech', and therefore it is true. What it states will surely come true.

Of Searle's speech-act categories the functions of the second (to assert, state) and fifth (to advise) are the most typical of these prayers. The clause formally reminds us much more of proverbs which also belong to the second and fifth categories. The proverb 'the early bird catches the worm' is just as much a statement as advice: get up early and you will catch the worm. It is the same as: say this prayer at night and in the morning and seven of your deadly sins will be forgiven. But while proverbs are validated 'only' by experience and ancient laws, these prayers are validated by God. They bear sacred validity.

Validity gained in Heaven ensures that these prayers are really effective and powerful. Since the Sacred Word, God's Word, is the guarantee, the success of the speech act is also guaranteed, and according to the Bible the Sacred Word *creates*. It creates its own realization. God's Word is power and reality which infallibly creates the effect God intends.

Epilogue

This is my interpretation of these texts and my interpretation of the way the people who use them interpret them. Nevertheless I am aware of the fact that getting an answer to the question of what these texts mean and what people believe they mean is a difficult task.

Based on my experiences I have found that the researcher's questions are often uninterpretable to the respondents, and the answers therefore often misleading. This is understandable: those performing the actions never ask themselves how they should interpret them and their verbalization. It is precisely by formulating the question that we point them in the direction of explaining their statements in some shape or form. In cases like this we find ourselves face to face with the closed archaic world concept which lacks the awareness of alternatives. This absence is the reason for the absolute assent of the

1. D. Hymes, 'The Ethnography of Speaking', in T. Gladwin and W.C. Sturtevant (eds.), *An Anthropology of Human Behaviour* (Washington, DC, 1962).

accepted theoretic doctrines and excludes even the possibility of doubting them. The accepted doctrines therefore compel those who believe in them, and it is this compelling force we refer to when we call these doctrines and the texts in which they are laid down 'sacred'. Or, as Habermas states, 'The life world conserves the interpretations of previous generations. It is the conservative balance as opposed to the risk of disagreeing which develops during the course of all timely reconciliation of views'.[1]

In my opinion archaic Hungarian folk prayers can be best interpreted as archaic world concepts where 'normative consensus' and the absolute authority of sanctity is prevalent. Concerning the use of language it is difficult to make the well-known semiotic distinction with satisfactory exactness between linguistic expression, its semantic content, and the referent, what the speaker refers to with the help of the expression. There is a magic relationship between things and their names and thus the boundaries between language and the world conceptually merge.

---

1.   J. Habermas, *A Theory of Communicative Action* (ed. M. Heller; Budapest, 1985), p. 36.

The Importance of Prayers
in the Study of the Cosmologies and Religious Systems
of Native Oral Cultures

Alessandro Lupo

In the oral tradition of non-literate peoples, the texts that concern superhuman beings and their powers or the relations between these beings and humankind are usually of the utmost importance. This is clear from the elaborate norms that almost everywhere minutely regulate their utterance and determine when they may or may not be pronounced. But it cannot be said that scholarly attention has focused equally on all the manifestations of the oral religious tradition. Sacred narrative (myth) has always been a subject of keen interest, by virtue of its ability to express in condensed and figurative form ethical values, etiological and taxonomic principles, the organizational system of the cosmos and how it can be subjected to human control, and the very identity of the society that produced it. The same cannot be said about the principal form of human communication with the supernatural, namely prayer.

At the dawn of the present century Marcel Mauss noted that the study of prayer was still confined to theologians and philosophers and remarked that 'prayer seems to be one of those facts that do not attract the attention of a scholar who has a scrupulous but not very deep attitude to science'.[1] With the passage of time and the enormous expansion of ethnological research, there has been a host of accounts of the texts of the prayers of native oral cultures, but as a corollary to studies of oral tradition generally rather than the result of using these texts for the purpose of increasing our knowledge and understanding

---

1. M. Mauss, 'La prière', in *Oeuvres*. I. *Les fonctions sociales du sacré* (Paris: Les Editions de Minuit, 1968), p. 370.

of the cosmological and religious systems they express.[1]

The study of religious beliefs still continues to be based essentially on observing ritual acts and paraphernalia and recording the description that the participants give scholars about what they think and do. A great amount of very useful knowledge has been accumulated in this way, but it has proved to be incomplete and distorted. Ritual gestures and objects—however close the bond may be between the idea that inspires them and the way they are enacted, and however eloquent the sign language in which they are formulated—still leave unexpressed an enormous part of traditional religious knowledge. These gestures and objects may well be eloquently evocative for those who share the same culture, but for that very reason they remain incomprehensible to the outside observer. Hence the incompleteness and obscurity of information obtained in this way. The verbal formulation of beliefs ought to transmit the more substantial part underlying the symbolic acts and objects, but this is always and necessarily vitiated by the conditions in which it occurs, in the course of conversation directed by the ethnographer.

Even before the scholar selects, critically re-elaborates and interprets the material he or she has gathered in this fashion—the activities that any analytic process always involves—the ethnographic interview itself is already affected by the distorting influence that the ethnographer's social and cultural 'otherness' produces on the form and content of the conversation he or she conducts. But aside from these obvious and unavoidable inconveniences, the main flaw of the ethnographic interview is that it misses an important part of what it is designed to learn and understand. Obviously the whole direction of the interview cannot be left to the unsystematic inspiration of the natives,[2] so there is a chance of losing all or part of what one does not have the imagination to ask and what they do not have the initiative to

1.   If anything, there has been greater interest in spells, incantations and magic formulas, where power over reality is attributed more to the force of the words themselves than to the beings mentioned. See B. Malinowski, *Coral Gardens and their Magic* (2 vols.; Bloomington: Indiana University Press, 1965), and S.J. Tambiah, 'The Magical Power of Words', *Man* NS 3.1 (1968), pp. 175-208.

2.   This is due to the fact that the ethnographic interview is actually a dialogue where information does not emerge spontaneously, but rather as a result of stimulation by one of the participants, 'directing' the conversation according to answers obtained in constant feedback.

say. The 'distance' of the eye the ethnologist turns to another culture is certainly indispensable in order to grasp that culture's particular features, to allow comparisons and to interpret function and meaning, but it also means that the interpretive grids he or she applies do not always fully cover the multiplicity of forms, uses and meanings of the reality he or she is observing.

The study of the religious beliefs and cosmological systems of oral tradition societies cannot ignore the fact that they have their being in the concrete realm of the actions, words and feelings of individuals much more than in the elaborate theoretical constructs of which they are the only perceptible manifestation. That is to say, they are indissolubly linked to the 'practical knowledge' of the people who deal every day with reality and with the culturally transmitted ways of facing it.[1] In order, therefore, to grasp the way that religious beliefs are independently organized, formulated and experienced by those who share them, it is necessary to study their practical application (primarily in ritual but also in iconography) and supplement and complete the observation of the acts they inspire by registering the words that accompany, justify and comment on those acts.

I am of the opinion that the oral texts used for ritual purposes provide the most eloquent and structured spontaneous formulation of native cosmological and religious knowledge, the essential documentary nucleus for supplementing the observation of ritual action and paraphernalia, and the fundamental element for comparing and corroborating the information collected in ethnographic interviews. They are the most fully ordered and linguistically rich form of traditional indigenous thought about the universe and the entities that rule it; and even more importantly, they are the form most immune from contamination by intercultural dialogue.

These texts generally take two forms. One is that of myth, where the origin and order of the cosmos, humankind and superhuman powers are represented in a narrative key, using a host of expressive registers and constantly resorting to metaphorical figures. Thus the 'sacred truths' are enunciated in highly evocative symbolic language. Mythic narrations are hard to understand for people from another culture who have difficulty penetrating the interlocking of their figurative meanings. In addition, these narratives often follow very

1. See B. Tedlock, *Time and the Highland Maya* (Albuquerque: University of New Mexico Press, 1982), p. 6.

slowly in the wake of the transformations of the context in which they were produced, the context to which they are elastically linked by bonds that may be subjected to abrupt acceleration and therefore slacken. Thus the dynamics of a society may be temporally out of step with their repercussions at the level of mythopoesis. Indeed, even among non-literate peoples, these narratives often fail to keep pace with the rapid and sometimes dramatic evolution of social and economic situations on which the impact of Western civilization imposes highly accelerated rhythms. One effect is that as time passes and the culture changes, faith in the founding message of the myths may weaken, and while the myths remain unchanged in their narrative form, they survive as legends, fables or simple folktales.[1]

This is not the case with prayer, which, with rare exceptions, always takes its start from the specific needs of the person formulating it, so that prayer has a distinctly utilitarian nature.[2] It is, by definition, the fruit of present reality and closely tied to the context of the ritual and the circumstances that give rise to it (a situation of need, suffering, transition, or the like). Hence prayer expresses religious belief in its concrete everyday dimension, and we can grasp how it is experienced, verbalized and 'acted out' by the natives. Moreover, even when it is an invocation that an individual extemporaneously addresses to the divinity, it never fails to reflect faithfully the design of the conceptual system that inspired it and the foundations of the faith of the person who utters it.

Prayer is unlike myth. A mythic narration can survive as an empty shell even when the truths it contained have crumbled; but prayer exists only on condition that the person who utters it believes in the existence of the entities he or she addresses, in the possibility of communicating with them, and in the possibility that they can act on the reality in which he or she lives. 'In some way every prayer is always a

---

1.   Of the numerous examples available, I would like to cite one I know personally: the ancient Mesoamerican myth of the origin of the sun and the moon, which has survived among the Huaves of the Isthmus of Tehuantepec in the form of a comical, obscene tale. See A. López Austin, *Los mitos del Teacuache* (Mexico City: Alianza Editorial Mexicana, 1990), p. 470.

2.   G. Calame Griaule notes that, among the Dogon, 'really disinterested prayers are rare' (*Ethnologie et langage: la parole chez les Dogon* [Paris: Gallimard, 1965], p. 412).

credo', as Mauss rightly observes.[1] This gives it extraordinary expressive power and also makes prayer an extremely reliable and representative testimony to the religious ideas of the person who utters it.

Ritual activities during which prayers are addressed to the super-natural are often a culture's last resort in attempting to remedy the difficulties of an existence that cannot be adequately controlled with the poor means—technical and conceptual alike—at the disposal of the natives. Side by side with a psychological need for some prospect of hope, there exists what I would call a 'cognitive' need to confer order on reality. This is the source of that effort to apply some form of culturally determined control even to those aspects of reality which are not fully within the range of action of what de Martino calls 'effective realistic behavior for facing the negative and reducing it to human dimension'.[2]

Prayer is the verbal expression that arises most directly from the inner experience of faith, and that is the reason for much of its heuristic value to scholars. Nor is this usefulness diminished by the fact that prayer arises from the idiosyncratic emotional responses of individuals to existential contingencies that by their nature are extremely variable, since these responses are always modelled on a fairly rigid system of beliefs provided by tradition and are channelled into already tested and shared forms of expression. The idea that prayer springs quite spontaneously from the inner being should not make us forget that its application, forms and contents are to some degree always carefully controlled, just because of the great importance and delicacy everywhere attributed to communication with the extra-human world.

Aside from the structural constants that make oral texts recogniz-able as prayers even when they come from traditions that may be extremely different (constants that derive from the very nature of prayer as a form of communication and consist in the need to identify the extra-human interlocutor and the person uttering the prayer and in transmitting an intelligible message), comparison of the many examples taken from a single oral culture shows that behind the countless variations, there is a circumscribable uniformity of style, content and use. Nor could it be otherwise. However different the

1. Mauss, 'La prière', p. 358.
2. E. de Martino, *Sud e magia* (Milan: Feltrinelli, 1987), p. 175.

names given to the main divinities within a single culture, it is impossible in any single case to confuse the one to whom an invocation is addressed (chosen because of the degree of control the particular divinity exercises over the sphere of interest of the person offering the prayer). In my experience with the Nahua Indians of the Sierra de Puebla in Mexico I have encountered therapeutic supplications in which different healers invoke a pair of divinities to whom they never give exactly the same name: for example María Nicolasa Trinidad and Juan Antonio Trinidad; María Santísima Trinidad del Mundo and Don Antonio Martín Marqués Domínica; Padre Trinidad and Madre Trinidad. But hidden behind these different appellatives there is always the same terrestrial duality, which is held responsible for somehow having appropriated a part of the soul of the ill person.[1]

Prayer is first of all (for the person who utters it) an act of communication, although most of the time it is one-way communication.[2] It is an act that presupposes that the person praying and the recipient of the prayer share the same language and that the two parties unerringly recognize each other. Hence the prayer is formulated in what is considered the most expressive and appropriate language and terminology,[3] and the superhuman interlocutor is always designated unequivocally by all his or her names, including any that may be esoteric, and his or her specific attributes and capabilities are acknowledged. This is why prayer is usually very descriptive and more

---

1.   An in-depth study of the beliefs, practices and prayers regarding the evils that, according to the Nahuas, oppress human souls can be found in I. Signorini and A. Lupo, *I tre cardini della vita: Anime, corpo, infermità tra i Nahua della Sierra di Puebla* (Palermo: Sellerio, 1989); other examples of Nahua prayer, and not only prayers for healing, are found in A. Lupo, 'L'oralità rituale dei Nahua della Sierra: Le concezioni cosmologiche di un gruppo indio messicano, studiate attraverso i testi religiosi tradizionali' (PhD thesis, La Sapienza University, Rome, 1990).

2.   In the sense that the response of the deity addressed rarely appears, when received at all, during the prayer itself, and almost never verbally: it is, for the most part, expressed in symbolic language through dreams, 'signs' and omens which always require interpretation (the origin of the various *-mancies*: oneiromancy, cleiromancy, etc.).

3.   In societies where several languages are spoken, it is rare to find that their use in the field of the sacred is not subject to distinctions, be they the so-called 'secret languages' (often restricted to this area) or bona fide ethnic languages, indigenous or introduced by colonialism.

explicit than myth. A few examples will suffice, all of them from the Nahua repertory.

In a long invocation for rain, the powers of St John the Baptist, lord of water and planting, are described as follows:

> You, St John the Baptist. . .
> You are the maker of water,
> You know where you keep water,
> You are the rightful lord of this water,
> Of the rivers,
> Of the great seas there.
> You are commanding them,
> You are keeping them. . .

On the occasion of a new hearth being set up, an invocation is made for the benevolent intervention of the main figures of the local syncretic pantheon, and the person uttering the prayer lists their names and attributes and describes their relationship to himself or herself and to people in general. (Unfortunately the wealth of symbols and the evocative power of the original is lost in translation):

> My Saviour Jesus Christ,
> Holy Trinity of the world,
> World of earth and water, surface of the earth, flat earth,
> Don Antonio Martín Marqués Domínica.
> (I) am in your lap, in your hands.
> In your sight I insistently ask a great boon.
> You hold me in your lap,
> With your right Hand,
> With your Foot.
> I want to set (here) this Antonio hearth,
> Spiral hearth of fire. . .
> Navel of fire,
> Saint Anthony of light.
> (I want it) to rest here,
> To place itself /sit/ here,
> That it may provide me with food,
> Provide me with drink
> For (all) the duration of my holy life. . .

Among other things, it is precisely when prayer describes the capabilities and spheres of action of the different superhuman entities that it frequently re-evokes myth, when explicitly or allusively referring to the events that gave birth to those entities. In another Nahua prayer the Baptist is invoked during corn planting, because an apocryphal myth says that it was at his behest that Christ created this crop:

> Lord St John the Baptist,
> You are the lord of this cane /the corn plant/
> You are the lord of this cane,
> You showed it /gave it to people/.
> You asked insistently our Father Jesus Christ,
> You asked for it insistently of Our Lord of work,
> You asked insistently for this seed.
> You have made us lords of it so that we may eat,
> We (who) are your children.[1]

Very rarely during ethnographic conversation does one hear so succinctly, exhaustively and expressively stated the fundamentals of indigenous theology and cosmology. But let me repeat that the greatest heuristic value of these formulations is that they are the altogether *spontaneous* product of the oral expressiveness of the natives, in full conformity with the design of their particular system of thought. This is why prayers sometimes contain lists of superhuman beings that may be studied as genuine verbal schematic depictions of their pantheon, arranged in a precise hierarchical order modelled after that of the human society. Consider in this regard one last Nahua example, in which a therapist invokes all the beings he believes can help to recover the lost soul of his patient:

> World of earth and water, flat earth,
> World of earth and water, surface of the earth.
> Saint John flat earth,
> Saint John surface of the earth,
> Saviour of the world.
> Father Trinity,
> Mother Trinity,
> Most Holy Trinity.
> José María Sacrament,
> José María Trinity.
> Juan Manuel Martín,
> Juan Manuel Antonio.
> Saint John Crescentius God,
> Saint John of light,

---

1. An example of a prayer containing an allusion to another apocryphal myth is given in A. Lupo, '"Tatiochihualatzin": Valores simbólicos del alcohol en la Sierra de Puebla', *Estudios de Cultura Nahuatl*, 21 (1991), pp. 224-26.

Morning star.
Mother of mine ancestress of *talocan*,[1]
Father of mine ancestor of *talocan*,
Holy gospels of *talocan*,
Saint John the Evangelist,
Holy Archangels.
Jesus Christ of *talocan*,
President of *talocan*,
(Town) councils of *talocan*,
Aldermen of *talocan*,
Policemen of *talocan*,
Officers of *talocan*,
Ushers of *talocan*.

The full wealth of information contained in prayers may not fully emerge in these brief fragments, but it can be investigated in the interview with the person reciting the prayer. Prayers like those of the Nahua offer a dual advantage—not otherwise evident in the prayers of literate peoples—of reproducing and expressing with extraordinary faithfulness the fundamentals of religious thought as it is experienced by the natives. And, aside from brief extemporary invocations that individuals may utter privately (and their unstructured immediacy makes them similar in all cultures), these prayers also have the dual value of sharing in the intrinsic mutability of oral texts while remaining subject to the iron laws of tradition.

Unlike written prayers, where the only freedom allowed is in the way the immutable text is interpreted,[2] prayers that are only transmitted orally are by nature bound to the contingencies of their utterance, the infinite variety of circumstances (environmental, economic, social, psychological and so on) in which they are recited. Indeed, most of the time they are not fixed texts learned by heart word for word but ephemeral compositions made up of pre-existing standardized 'pieces' combined and arranged in different patterns depending on the

1. With *talocan* today's Nahuas do not mean to imply an exact equivalence with the ancient pre-Hispanic Tlalocan, the verdant, heavenly eastern domain of the rain god Tlaloc, but rather the nether world, not to be confused with the Christian hell, known as *mictan*, 'the place of the dead' (see Signorini and Lupo, *I tre cardini della vita*, p. 173).
2. 'Readings' of the *Our Father*, for example, have constantly followed changes in doctrine in the various Christian confessions (see Mauss, 'La prière', p. 488).

circumstances in a kind of linguistic patchwork.[1] The flexibility, truthfulness, and immediacy with which oral prayers reflect the multi-faceted nature of religious thought as it is experienced in life are particularly evident where (as among the Nahua) both forms of prayer exist, written and oral. The core of communication with the supernatural is in the oral prayer, while the written prayer is used almost exclusively as a testimony of faith and, almost like a mute object, it is offered up in the same way as candles or flowers.[2]

Prayer texts which have been created and used only orally, and which have been accepted, used and transmitted in the course of time, are those that have gone through rigid screening and won the approval of the group. I would call this an almost 'technical' consequence of what Goody calls 'the tendency of oral cultures towards cultural homeostasis', so that 'the innumerable mutations of culture that emerge in the ordinary course of verbal interaction are either adopted by the interacting group, or they get eliminated in the process of transmission from one generation to the next'.[3] In this context prayers must fully meet the requirements of representing the religious thought of the members of a community, and they must not deviate from the feelings shared by the community, so that any innovative or conservative peaks of individuals are flattened out and elided by the censure or disinterest of the majority.[4] A comparable mechanism applies a strong rein to individual drives in the direction of heterodoxy and endows prayer with a capacity to illustrate with extraordinary fidelity the elements and structures of the indigenous system of religious thought.

Hence the seeming contradiction of texts that are constantly adapted

---

1.   Cf. Lupo, 'L'oralità rituale dei Nahua della Sierra'. None of this differs substantially from A.B. Lord, *The Singer of Tales* (Cambridge, MA: Harvard University Press, 1960), pp. 33, 43 (quoted in J. Goody, *The Domestication of the Savage Mind* [Cambridge: Cambridge University Press, 1977], p. 117) regarding the art of the singer, who 'cannot, and does not, remember enough to sing a song: he must, and does, learn to create phrases. So phrases get "adjusted"; there is no rigidity in what he hears, and certainly none in what he does'.

2.   See Signorini and Lupo, *I tre cardini della vita*, pp. 170-74.

3.   Goody, *Domestication of the Savage Mind*, p. 14.

4.   Although I am considering community consensus, I am taking for granted that even in more culturally homogeneous societies, there are individuals who reach a higher level of competency in religious matters and are the ones allowed, more or less institutionally, to innovate or approve, as long as this does not spill over into heterodoxy, the reaction to which is either isolation or oblivion.

to changing society and culture yet maintain intact vestiges of the forms of an ancient past.[1] What matters is that for the scholar who collects and studies prayers, they are always an 'instrument that functions'—not so much from the perspective (*emic*) of the natives, that prayers are meant to obtain something from a divinity, but rather from the perspective (*etic*) of scholars: prayers can satisfy the often unconscious needs (cognitive, psychological, social) of the people who utter them.

1.   Again, I have in mind today's Nahuatl supplications bestowing Catholic saints with the same appellations as pre-Hispanic native deities (for example the fire saint Anthony, still referred to as *lamatzin*, 'old Woman', a term in use at the time of the Conquest with reference to the god of fire [see H. Ruiz de Alarcón, *Treatise on the Heathen Superstitions and Customs that Today Live among the Indians Native to this New Spain* (ed. J.R. Andrews and R. Hassig; Norman, OK: University of Oklahoma Press, 1984), pp. 167, 228]). I am also thinking about certain public prayers intoned by Huave ritualists, who continue to call the town hall *real juzgado*, 'royal court', more than 150 years after independence from the Spanish crown, invoking the divinities whose images once resided therein, and transferred to the church decades ago.

Part 3: Sociology

Introduction to Part 3: Sociology

Jon Davies and Isabel Wollaston

In the third section of the book two of our contributors (Mark Chapman and Loren Pfister) deal explicitly with Max Weber, while the third (Kathleen Thomas), in her analysis of the various formulations of the Quaker *Book of Discipline*, by implication follows a Weberian line in relating theological to social changes. Mark Chapman's essay on the early nineteenth-century Chicago Divinity School, headed by Shailer Matthews, is an analysis of another form of 'action theology', as the leading academic divines of the great and greatly turbulent city of Chicago tried to apply their religious beliefs to the social problems of one of the fastest growing cities in the world. Like so many academics who step forth into the political market place, Shailer had to confront the question posed by Max Weber: 'which of the warring Gods are we to serve?'—the self-evidently successful capitalist God of Individualism, or the God of the Beatitudes? For Weber the essential tragedy of the West—its Iron Cage—lay in the fact that nothing other than the power of the market seemed to be involved in the formulation of the answer to the question. Money procured the theology it wanted, and the moral prescriptions of a religion which originated in notions of 'community' were forced further and further back into a kind of privatized bemusement, watching in horror the huge success of capitalism in creating an engine of seemingly endless material profusion. In Chicago, academics in both the Divinity School and in the great School of Sociology sought to derive from their two disciplines an ethic of community, of co-operative civic practices to contend with the evident victims of the great onrushing potencies of urbanization and proletarianization represented in the growth of Chicago. They essentially failed; Mayor Daley succeeded.

From the other side of the world Lauren Pfister of the Hong Kong

Baptist College provided the conference with a detailed analysis of Max Weber's Confucian and Puritan forms of rationalism. Weber was of the view that Confucianism, as expressed in the traditions of Imperial China's intellectual class, had a quietist rationality, leading to 'rational adjustment to the world', whereas Puritanism (as exemplified in Chicago?) was either committed to or led to 'rational mastery of the world'. Pfister shows that the relationship between Confucian doctrines and practices, and their interactions with the State, did indeed produce a 'Canon' with clear (but varying) sociological functions; at the very least, it would be hard to imagine the Empire being quite so long-lived had Calvin gone to Peking rather than Geneva! In China, sacred texts and civil service etiquette clearly worked for the State; and Pfister's essay shows not only how text and etiquette informed and transformed each other over the history of the Empire, but also how the very business of translating these texts *for the benefit of the West* was itself in part determined by the concerns and interests of the newly-dominant Western empires of Europe and America. These trans-cultural imperial interests, inside and outside China, created a kind of 'league table' of canonical texts, with periodic promotions and demotions, and the occasional relegation. This is clearly not a finished process.

Kathleen Thomas's work immediately puts us onto a very different scale; Quakers are few in number—perhaps 200,000 in the world. As a Civil War-derived sect (the 'English' Civil War that is), the Quakers have an archive founded in the era of the printing press, and as an unusually methodical people they have texts, semi-canonical if not sacred, which are changed to the accompaniment of carefully stated reasons: little needs to be tendentiously inferred from or imputed to the text-changers of the Religious Society of Friends! Kathleen Thomas's paper charts the steady alteration in the substance and style of a religious movement gradually abandoning the stance of being 'in the world but not of it'. Sacred texts, as insisted-upon truths, are the boundary markers of religious groups, the available 'test' of membership; and as boundary markers they will change their canonical status as the group comes to regard the very maintenance of boundaries as being more of a hindrance than a help, or as the group members come to feel less threatened by 'the world'. This paper raises at least two interesting questions: is it, contrary to common sense, perhaps easier to change a written text than to change an oral tradition; and do sacred texts which are changed in order to make accommodations with the world thereby lose their social as well as sacred function?

Reassessing Max Weber's Evaluation
of the Confucian Classics

Lauren Pfister

The year that Max Weber began his studies on the economic ethics of
the world religions, 1911, was also the year of the collapse of the
Qing empire.[1] Five or six years later, when Weber began to publish
the results of his labours on Confucianism, Taoism and other religions, Republican China had already endured an unsuccessful attempt
by the first President, Yuan Shika, to initiate a new dynasty. Before
Weber's death in 1920 China had been transformed further from its
traditional moorings through the May Fourth Movement. This event
in 1919 prompted, among many other precedents among intellectuals,
the intitiative to replace all classical forms of writing still embedded
in educational curricula with vernacular texts. Already in 1905 the
civil service examinations, which for hundreds of years had employed
the Confucian Classics (with their attendant classical writing forms) as
the standard curriculum, had been cancelled by imperial decree. The
additional steps taken during the May Fourth Movement, moving
China even further away from its traditional cultural roots, were
greeted as genuine progress toward adopting more scientific and
democratic institutions for Republican China.

In this historical setting Weber, referring to the traditional
Confucian education system, wrote: 'This education was transmitted
only through the study of the old classics, whose absolutely canonical
prestige and purified forms of orthodoxy went without question'.[2] In
the following two pages, Weber summarized his view of the
'significance of the Classics': they were in his mind the results of a

---

1. See M. Weber, *The Sociology of Religion* (trans. E. Fishchoff; Beacon
Press, 1964), pp. 275-79.
2. M. Weber, *The Religion of China* (trans. H. Garth; Free Press, 1964), p. 163.

'relentless canonization of tradition'.[1] Although the actual process of establishing these Confucian texts as the unquestionable authoritative standards was only decided, according to Weber, by the 'eighth century of the Christian era',[2] the economic and social conditions of the varying dynasties caused imperial China to use the texts as a means to social stability and the support of the imperial hierarchy.

One must credit Weber for having recognized the fact that there were Confucian literati who 'consult[ed] Antiquity about problems of the present' and came up with answers antagonistic to the currently accepted norms.[3] Nevertheless Weber and others have continued to insist that these were unusual cases, always and ultimately ineffective against the strongholds of Confucian traditionalism.

In the more than seventy years since Weber published these views, the Confucian canon has fallen from its institutionalized authoritative role like a burning meteorite. A public memorial to this demise seems to be underscored by Harold Coward in his recent book, *Sacred Word and Sacred Text*; there is not even a single mention of the Confucian tradition and its texts as religious.[4]

In this paper I will argue that the case for the nature and social function of the Confucian texts in traditional Chinese culture is more complex than Weber and others have suggested. It is complicated by a number of unresolved tensions in the understanding of the texts and their context, all of which are recognized and debated by contemporary scholars. The nature of the crisis surrounding the contemporary significance of the Confucian Classics, I will argue, can only be manifest once this more complex picture is understood.

Weber's Theses

Fundamental to Weber's evaluation of Confucianism was his well-known comparison between Confucian and Puritan forms of rationalism: the former provided 'rational adjustment to the world', the latter, 'rational mastery of the world'.[5] When Weber typified Confucianism

---

1.   Weber, *Religion of China*, p. 164.

2.   Weber, *Religion of China*, p. 165.

3.   Weber, *Religion of China*, pp. 163-64.

4.   See H. Coward, *Sacred Word and Sacred Text: Scripture in World Religions* (Maryknoll: Orbis Books, 1988).

5.   Weber, *Religion of China*, p. 218, and *idem*, *Sociology of Religion*, p. 270.

as a form of religiosity, he followed Hegel's assessment in claiming it to be 'a belief in spirits or simply a belief in magic, [its] ethics [being] no more than a clever accommodation to the world on the part of the educated man'.[1] Confucian spirituality was a religion for the upper class, the literati, feeding its particular form of self control with a 'dis-esteem for plebian irrationality'.[2]

Historical evidence can be produced to support these claims, but it is now questioned whether or not they are, as Weber wanted to assert, the most important characteristics of Confucianism throughout its long history. These challenges to Weber's basic theses on Confucianism can be characterized by three tensions: the tension between historical actuality and canonical content; the tension between radical traditionalism and forms of self-cultivation; and the tension between institutional mechanisms of control and intellectual autonomy. Before pursuing the qualifications to Weber's claims which become evident once these tensions in the Confucian tradition are recognized, there is one further challenge to Weber's assumptions which must be addressed.

Weber's Fundamental Assumption

Easily the most basic assumption to Weber's research was that Confucianism is a religion, containing a particular form of spiritual piety, expressed through rituals and ethics which illustrate its 'this-worldly' form of religiosity. Certainly Weber was not alone in making this kind of assessment: Enlightenment philosophers in Europe believed they had found in Confucianism a 'natural religion', a spirituality built exclusively out of the resources native to all humanity. Their information had been interpreted from the reports of Jesuit missionaries, some of whom identified within the ancient Confucian Classics hints of a kind of monotheism.[3] Later descriptions of the state cult seemed to confirm the existence of a thoroughly institutionalized

---

The success of the Pacific Rim economies has by some analysts been associated with the influence of Confucian ethics, raising further doubt about the validity of Weber's argument.

1. See G.W.F. Hegel, *Lectures on the Philosophy of Religion* (ed. P. Hodgson, trans. R.F. Brown; Berkeley: University of California Press, 1988), pp. 235-50.
2. Weber, *Sociology of Religion*, p. 255.
3. See for example M. Ricci, *The True Meaning of The Lord of Heaven* (*T'ien-chu Shih-i*) (trans. D. Lancashire and P. Hu Kuo-chen, Ricci Institute, 1985).

worship of the Sovereign Lord (*Shangdi*) along with other cosmic, natural and ancestral spirits.[1]

A strong reaction against identifying Confucianism as a religion grew up among Catholic and Protestant missionaries who dealt with living Confucian literati and read the commentaries of the Confucian classics written by orthodox Confucians. The philosophical tenets of the Confucian works of the Song dynasty (9960–1290), which had become the standards for the orthodox interpretation of Confucianism by the middle of the fourteenth century, were believed to be atheistic by some Jesuit scholars. Intellectuals of the French Academy in Paris had at first included various Confucian Classics among the sacred books of the Orient,[2] but by the end of the nineteenth century there had been a reversal. One academician claimed that because Confucianism had no revealed doctrines and was mainly concerned about mundane affairs, it was below all forms of religion and should only be considered a teaching of men.[3] Already low in the hierarchy of world religions, Confucianism was demoted to being not religious in character.

This opposition has persisted till the present day, and has been extended now to include scholars in China and its Asian neighbours, as well as sinologists in Western academic circles. Some argue that Confucianism is not religious at all, that the very category of 'religion' is foreign to Confucian thought, and that it should be rec-

---

1.   The description of various aspects of the Imperial religion, including lengthy translations of prayers recited by the Emperor, are found in J. Legge, *The Religions of China: Confucianism and Taoism Described and Compared with Christianity* (London: Hodder & Stoughton, 1880). See also W.E. Soothill, *The Three Religions of China* (Oxford: Oxford University Press, 2nd edn, 1923); and L. Thompson, 'Confucian Thought: The State Cult', in M. Eliade (ed.), *The Encyclopedia of Religion* (London: Macmillan, 1987).

2.   In *Les Livres Sacres de l'Orient* (Paris, 1840), M.G. Pauthier translated the *Book of Documents*, the Neo-Confucian *Four Books* and a note on the *Book of Changes* in the very front of all the other selections, including the Qur'an and the Laws of Manu. Republished in 1852, with versions of *The Analects* and *The Mencius* published separately in 1854, these texts had a large influence on European readership. It is significant that the books are described as 'sacred' and that only two of the five Chinese Classics are included among them.

3.   These comments were made in a review of the *Sacred Books of China* translated by James Legge for F.M. Müller's series The Sacred Books of the East by B.-S. Hilaire, *Journal des Savants* (1894), pp. 513-20.

ognized only as a philosophical school.[1] Marxist scholars in the People's Republic of China have argued that Confucianism displayed many religious attitudes and promoted many religious beliefs in its long history. This is done, of course, in order to cast it aside as an ultimately unsatisfying form of feudal ideology.[2] Still others, notably among Western sinologists or Chinese scholars in Western universities, want to revitalize the religious core of Confucianism stripped of its feudal past. Relying on different classics and different Confucian representatives, they point out a variety of ways to conceive of Confucian religion. Some include a more humanistic, everyday form of religious seriousness;[3] others refuse to reduce the transcendence described in the Classics, arguing that there is an authentic dialogue with the transcendent in Confucianism.[4]

The Confucian Canon

At this point it is worth asking for more details regarding the nature and authority of the Confucian scriptures. In doing so one may come to several important conclusions. First, the processes of the canonization and extension of the Confucian scriptures have direct relationships to specific historical contexts as well as particular religious and philosophical questions. Secondly, the general openness of the Confucian canon, permitting a variety of interpretations despite standardizations reinforced in various periods, leads one to a very different understanding of Confucianism than that described by Max Weber. Finally, it can provide some insight into the reasons for the unsettled question as to whether or not Confucianism is a religious tradition.

In order to deal with the complexities involved in the nature and authority of the Confucian canon, Weber had access to one source which is still an invaluable resource for Confucian studies: the exten-

1. A recently published text on this issue is R. Eno's *The Confucian Creation of Heaven: Philosophy and the Defence of Ritual Mastery* (New York: State University of New York Press), 1990.

2. See Ren Jiyu[ag], 'On the Formation of Confucian Religion' *Chinese Social Sciences* 1 (1980), pp. 61-74.

3. See Mou Zongsan[ah], *The Special Characteristics of Chinese Philosophy* (Taipei Student Bookshop, 1982), pp. 89-101.

4. See in particular Tu Weiming[ai], *Centrality and Commonality: An Essay on Confucian Religiousness* (New York: State University of New York Press), 1989.

sive translations and commentaries prepared by James Legge (1815–1897), a missionary in Hong Kong for the London Missionary Society (1843–1873), and later the first Professor of Chinese Language and Literature at Corpus Christi College in Oxford (1876–1897).[1] Legge made it his life's goal to make authoritative translations and commentaries of the Confucian Classics, beginning the first set of publications in 1861 and completing the last one in 1885.[2] His self-conscious procedure in setting out the plans for the translations is very suggestive with regard to the problem of the religious nature of the Confucian texts. A second and very recent work by John Henderson entitled *Scripture, Canon, and Commentary: A Comparison of Confucian and Western Exegesis*[3] provides a wealth of data from which the complexity of Confucian traditions can be summarized.

In his extensive prolegomenon to each translation, Legge provided encyclopaedic information regarding the content and reliability of each of the Confucian Classics. This included a chronological overview of the varying stages of canonization.[4] Great sociological importance should be placed on the fact that Legge did not publish the texts in the order of their historical appearance. The first texts published were *The Four Books* (*Sishu*), comprising *The Analects* (*Lunyu*), *The Mencius* (*Menqzi*) and two chapters of the Confucian Classic called *The Books of Rites* (*Liji*): *The Great Learning* (*Daxue*) and *The Doctrine of the Mean* (*Zhong-yong*). These texts were the nucleus of works first set apart as a unit by the Song dynasty scholar Zhu Xi (1130–1200). The first two texts—*The Analects* and *The Mencius*—had become important sources for information about Confucius, but were not part of the earliest and most ancient Chinese scriptures. The latter two texts functioned, according to Zhu Xi, in different ways. *The Great Learning* was the text to master as one

1. See my study, 'The Failures of James Legge's Fruitful Life for China', in *Ching Feng[ai]* 13.4 (Dec. 1988), pp. 246-71.

2. Legge's translations of the Confucian Classics were well known to Max Weber. See my articles in *The Sino–Western Cultural Relations Journal* 12 (1990), pp. 29-50 and 13 (1991), pp. 33-46.

3. J. Henderson, *Scripture, Canon and Commentary: A Comparison of Confucian and Western Exegesis* (Princeton, NJ: Princeton University Press, 1991).

4. See J. Legge, *The Chinese Classics with a Translation, Critical and Exegetical Notes, Prologomena and Copious Notes* (Oxford: Oxford University Press, 2nd edn, 1893), pp. 1-11.

began the route toward living a Confucian way. It set out the moral commitments and method of self-cultivation which was to be followed until one had reached sagehood. *The Doctrine of the Mean* depicted the final steps toward sageliness, and so was the most metaphysically and spiritually oriented of the four.

Zhu's aggressive approach to the problems of locating the heartbeat of the vast Confucian teachings available in his day was not immediately acceptable to his contemporaries. His childhood included memories of the results of the breakdown of the extended Song kingdom (the so-called Northern Song, 960–1127); the ever present threat of a Mongol invasion causing the final destruction of the Song dynasty stimulated an intense search for self-orientation and political equilibrium. *The Four Books* provided answers for these profound questions, even though in the case of *The Great Learning* Zhu Xi had taken extra effort to reorganize the text because of the common understanding by a number of Song Confucianists that this text had been corrupted.[1] Many of the battles later Neo-Confucians had to fight turned on the disruption of the text of *The Great Learning*, and the consequent distortion of its meaning which was meant to lead one toward sagehood.[2]

Legge had to translate *The Four Books* first because they had become the most basic Confucian texts employed in the civil service examinations. Ironically, the canonization of *The Four Books* as the orthodox interpretation of Confucianism came after Zhu's fears were realized. Several generations after his death, the Mongols did conquer the rest of the Song territories. Preferring Tibetan forms of Buddhism to all the Chinese alternatives, the Mongolian rulers only slowly gained an appreciation for the Confucian tradition. Gradually they were convinced that the re-establishment of the civil service examinations would assist the ruling of the empire. Consequently, disciples of Zhu Xi were able to convince the Mongolian emperor of the value of their teacher's commentaries for this purpose. Once established, these texts became the main (but not always the exclusive)

---

1. See D.K. Gardner, *Chu Hsi and The Ta-hseuh: Neo-Confucian Reflections on the Confucian Canon* (Cambridge, MA: Harvard University Press, 1986), pp. 1-60.

2. See J. Ching, *To Acquire Wisdom: The Way of Wang Yangming* (New York: Columbia University Press), 1976.

texts for the examinations.[1] The next texts Legge translated were the
most often quoted historical and literary texts of the Confucian
Classics. These were, in the order of their publication, *The Book of
Documents* in 1865 (*Shujing* or *Shangshu*), *The Book of Odes* com-
pleted in 1869 (*Shijing*), and the *Spring and Autumn Annals*
(*Chunqiu*) with notes from the *Zuo Commentary*[2] in 1872
(*Zuozhuan*). These were all part of the five Chinese Classics (*Wujing*),
the first two being employed by Confucius as standards for his own
cultivation, while the *Spring and Autumn Annals* was traditionally
believed to have been written by Confucius himself.[3] The first two
provided the standards for religious, ethical and cultural expressions;
the first and last became the standards for Chinese historical records
of the sage-kings and the destruction of less worthy rulers who came
before and after them.

Although these texts include materials dating back to the second
millennium BC, they were not taken as standards of scholarship until
the time of Confucius (551–479). These standards were not general-
ized and accepted as Classical authorities until 479 BC, well into the
Han dynasty (206 BC–AD 22). The Han emperor, who decided to
utilise the five Confucian Classics (including the three texts already
mentioned as well as *The Book of Changes* [*Ijing*] and *The Book of
Rites* [*Liji*] as the standards for government and grooming literati as
bureaucrats, was not exclusively attracted to Confucianism. Han Wudi
(Han Emperor Wu) was attracted to anything which would extend his
life and consolidate his kingdom. Undoubtedly, he considered the
teachers of these classics 'experts in the cultural and religious heritage
of the past', the *royal* past which Wudi intended to extend.[4] Only later

---

1.   See I. Miyazaki, *China's Examination Hell: The Civil Service Examinations
of Imperial China* (Weatherill, 1976).

2.   Legge included a complete translation of both the *Spring* and *Autumn Annals*
and the *Zuo Commentary*, which was the specific commentary Zhu Xi had favoured
in his study of this classic.

3.   See *The Mencius*, 3B.9, in Legge's *The Chinese Classics*, II, p. 283.

4.   See B. Schwartz, *The World of Thought in Ancient China* (Cambridge, MA:
Harvard University Press, 1985), pp. 374-78.

did the strong hand of the Confucian bureaucrat begin to be felt in Han China.[1]

Gradually new texts were added to this selective group of canonical texts. Legge mentions a list of Classics including nine texts, adding to the five already cited, two other texts on rites and two other commentaries to the *Spring and Autumn Annals*. By the period of the Tang dynasty (618–907) a list including thirteen texts was considered to include all the authoritative classics. These added to the nine already mentioned Confucius' *Analects, The Mencius, The Classic of Filial Piety* (*Xiaojing*), and the *Erya*, an important and ancient dictionary.[2] Henderson has found one Qing dynasty scholar who counted 21 texts as classics (*jing*).[3]

The addition of these final four texts has very much to do with the Confucian encounter with Daoist masters and Buddhist monks. The great Confucian literary master Han Yu (768–824) was the first to attempt to overcome the great attractiveness of Buddhist metaphysics and Daoist longevity. It was he who became noted for singling out *The Great Learning* and *The Doctrine of the Mean* as texts offering better means of understanding the world and life than the methods of the Buddhists or Daoists. His strict fundamentalism also included the first list of 'orthodox' Confucians, by this means bringing *The Analects* and *The Mencius* into great prominence.[4] From this religious background it is not difficult to see how the Song scholars could adopt Han Yu's suggestions, providing their own solutions to the challenges of Buddhism and Daoism, and so lead (as in Zhu Xi's work) to the pre-eminent status of *The Four Books*.

Only after going to Oxford did Legge have the opportunity to complete his translations of the Chinese classics. There was at this point an important departure from earlier translations in both form and motivation. His colleague F. Max Müller arranged for Legge to do a set of translations for his series The Sacred Books of the East, including four volumes of all the religious portions of the Confucian Classics as well as two volumes of the major and representative texts

1. See Henderson, *Scripture, Canon, and Commentary*, pp. 38-50.
2. See Legge, *The Chinese Classics*, I, pp. 2-3.
3. See Henderson, *Scripture, Canon, and Commentary*, pp. 49-50.
4. See C. Hartman, *Han Yu and the Tang Search for Unity* (Princeton, NJ: Princeton University Press, 1986).

from the Daoist tradition.[1] The first volume of these *Sacred Books of China* appeared in 1879 and included a retranslation of the whole of the *Book of Documents*, selected portions of *The Book of Odes*, and *The Classic of Filial Piety*. The reappearance of the first two texts in this religious context indicates to what extent, at least in Legge's broad understanding, the Chinese classics constituted religiously authoritative texts. In the introduction to this volume, the reader discovers that Legge was intensely concerned about the place of God (*Shangdi/di*) in *The Book of Documents* and *The Book of Odes*. Not only did he support his translation of the term relevant to this topic, but he even reorganized the selection of *The Book of Odes* so that the sections which were predominantly related to the Sovereign Lord came first (rather than their traditional place at the end of the text).[2] Later, in 1882, *The Book of Changes* was published along with most of its classical commentaries, some of which were traditionally believed to be authored by Confucius. Finally, the massive text of *The Book of Rites* was published in two volumes in 1885. In his introduction, Legge provided summaries of each of the 46 chapters of the classical text, thereby highlighting those materials which were particularly significant for religious studies.

The religious significance of these translations, especially in the light of Weber's assumption about Confucian religion, can now be brought into perspective. Rather than the whole of the canon, only selected texts, and in some cases selections within texts, could be appropriately described as religious. Matters of emphasis within the canon, therefore, could very well determine how religious a Confucian scholar might be. For example, the divinitory function (normally associated with *The Book of Changes* in later Confucian traditions) was highlighted in the 'Great Plan' (*Hongfan*) of *The Book of Documents*,[3] but in the whole of *The Analects* Confucius made only

1.   *The Sacred Books of China* appear as vols. 3, 16, 27-28 and 39-40 in the series The Sacred Books of the East. The last two are the Daoist volumes.

2.   The question of the presence of God in these religious classics was of great importance to Legge: see for example his *Letter to Professor Max Muller on the Translation into English of the Chinese Term Ti and Shang Ti* (London: Trubner & Co., 1880).

3.   See Weber, *Religion of China*, p. 165, and Legge, *The Chinese Classics*, I, p. 200.

one reference to that divinitory classic.[1] A contemporary scholar who emphasized the study of *The Four Books* might easily overlook the role of *The Book of Changes*, while a student of the *Five Classics* would not be able to avoid it.

Three general conclusions should be recognized at this point. First, the historical contexts of the canonization and development of the Confucian Classics in the Han, Tang, Song and Yuan dynasties (roughly 11th century BCE, and 7th, 12th and 14th century CE respectively) emphasized various religious roles in which the Confucian texts operated. Undoubtedly there were other ways in which they were employed, but the religious dimension is unavoidably prominent in each case.

Secondly, especially with regard to the Song scholar Zhu Xi and the text of *The Great Learning*, it is simply not the case that the canonicity and orthodoxy of the Confucian Classics 'went without question'. There were severe and long debates over the reliability of certain texts, with shifts in emphasis onto other Classics, and in some cases even the addition of new texts into the canon in order to consolidate new positions. This conclusion suggests that there were even more troublesome problems in the historical reliability of the texts—which in fact was the case. (The major debate which began in the Han dynasty and erupted with new fury in the Ming and Quing dynasties was known as the Old and New Text controversy.)[2] Another challenge to the functional importance of the Chinese Classics came as a result of the unconventional options in self-cultivation developed by the Ming dynasty scholar Wang Yangming (1472–1527) and others. They ultimately believed the Classics to be helpful but not necessary for attaining sagehood.[3]

Finally, openness and diversity of the Confucian canon permitted Confucianists at various times and in different contexts either to

---

1.   See *Analects* 7.16, and Legge, *The Chinese Classics*, I, p. 200, and *The Sacred Books of China, Part 3* (The Sacred Books of the East, 16; Oxford: Oxford University Press, 1882), pp. 1-2.

2.   The Old and New Test Controversy involves political issues and possible forgeries made to support the overturning of the Western Han dynasty, and whatever the truth of this, the fact remains that different traditions of the Classical texts have existed since the Han period.

3.   See earlier footnote.

emphasize or de-emphasize the religious or spiritual dimensions of the
Confucian Classics. As Henderson puts it:

> Chinese Confucianism is nearly unique…in its possession of a distinctly
> multi-book canon of very diverse origins… This perhaps made it easier to
> argue that the Confucian Classics were comprehensive, or at least they
> covered a wide range… Confucian commentators were less concerned
> with reconciling apparent contradictions in their canon than were
> Vedantists or biblical exegetes. One possible explanation for this is that
> the Confucian canon, especially the Five or Six Classics, is so diverse that
> points of conflict were not so conspicuous… When such questions arose,
> most Confucian commentators sought reconciliation, attempting to
> establish that the ideas of the ancient sages were really in harmony with
> one another.[1]

---

1.   Henderson, *Scripture, Canon, and Commentary*, pp. 100, 121-22.

Theology and Ethics:
The Principle of Fraternity in Shailer Mathews and Max Weber

Mark D. Chapman

1. *Sociology and Divinity in Chicago*

Writing in 1895 Albion Small, Head Professor in the first American Sociology Department founded at Chicago in 1892, remarked that the modern world was the 'era of sociology' (Small 1895: 1). In its early years, however, 'American sociology was chiefly an experimentation with method' (Small 1916: 788), and Small fought for a sociology which was not merely 'an impulse to improve ways of interpreting the world' but also 'an impulse to improve ways of improving the world' (Small 1916: 828). Thus he wrote in 1910: 'The primary and chief function of science is to act as all men's proxy in finding out all that can be known about what sort of a world this is, and what we can do in it to make life most worth living' (Small 1910: 260).

In Chicago, which had increased in population from 4000 in 1840 to 1,700,000 in 1900, and where the horrors of early capitalism were so blatant, 'the founders of sociology, with their generally nonurban and nonsecular experiences, were particularly sensitive to these problems' (Hinkle and Hinkle 1954: 16), and sociology was entrusted with the task of determining the limits and conditions of possible human action as the precondition for the amelioration of social problems. It was this ethical aspect of sociology, 'its highest power' (Small 1916: 854), which was pursued in the early days of the Chicago Department with an almost missionary zeal that set it apart from competing theories of self-interest and mere utilitarian schemes of social improvement (Small 1907). Small thus became 'truly a pioneer in the foundation of the sociological attitude toward ethics' (Barnes 1948: 791; cf. Dibble 1975: 153).

Sociology, Theology and Ethics

This moral impulse was reflected in the university itself which, although a Baptist foundation, under the guidance of its first president, William Harper and its benefactor, John D. Rockerfeller Sr, deliberately sought to be above denomination in the hope that free research would lead to a realistic and scientific approach to practical problems (Bulmer 1984: 24). The dissertations presented in the first years of the Sociology Department clearly illustrate this close connection between the theoretical and the practical, between sociology and social reform, and indeed between sociology and the churches (cf. Faris 1970: 12-13).

Chicago sociology was dominated, at least in its early years, by practising Christians and saw itself as the new science of religion in succession to theology, as nothing less than 'the holiest sacrament open to men'. In the same way Charles Henderson, who both taught sociology and was university chaplain, and who adopted a thoroughgoing empirical and statistical approach to sociology, could write that 'to assist us in the difficult task of adjustment to new situations God has providentially wrought for us the social sciences and placed them at our disposal' (Charles Henderson, cited in Bulmer 1984: 35). In a sense, then, the early sociologists saw themselves as the secular clergy of the new world.

If Christianity was a vital factor in the formation of the distinctive Chicago sociological position, so the sociological approach shaped the characteristic attitude of the Divinity School, which President Harper intended as 'a central scientific school of religion in place of a traditional seminary' (Ames 1959: 172). Religion was to be studied impartially and scientifically in an atmosphere of guaranteed academic freedom (cf. Mathews 1909). Theology would thus have to abdicate its crown as queen of the sciences in favour of a sociology which seemed to provide a possible escape route from a 'private Protestantism' which relegated religion to the sphere of 'personal salvation', where clergymen, who had so often been at the forefront of social reform in the past, now had 'to defer meekly to far more affluent vestrymen'. The move to sociology can be viewed as 'an attempt to restore through secular leadership some of the spiritual influence and authority and social prestige that clergymen had lost through the upheaval in the system of status and the secularization of society' (Hofstadter 1955: 151-52). In this way it could heal the 'rift between scientific theology and the rank and file of church members' (Mathews 1936: 42).

Beyond its strictly scientific concern, however, the Divinity School was also encouraged to develop 'a policy of maintaining a relationship with organised church life' (Mathews 1936: 58). In this it reflected the combination of theory and practice of the Sociology Department which became known as Harper's 'dialectic' (see Hynes 1981: ch. 1). This was later summarized by Shailer Mathews: 'In the early days of Chicago we felt ourselves to be something more than observers or critics of conventional church life. We had a Cause, the extension of correct, and as we believed, inspiring views of the Bible. We could not be cloistered scholars; we were to serve a religious movement' (Mathews 1936: 72).

The remainder of this paper charts the course of the conception of social individuality, more usually called 'fraternity', which was the guiding ethical principle of the early Chicago sociologists, in relation to the Chicago Divinity School with special reference to the most important figure in the development of the sociohistorical interpretation of the New Testament, Shailer Mathews, who was its dean from 1908–33.[1] What will be seen is that Mathews derives the ethical ideal of fraternity from the teachings of a Christ viewed as the proto-sociologist: it was Jesus himself who served to legitimize the fraternal goals of an ameliorative sociology. Finally, a brief comparison with the role of the biblical principle of fraternity in Max Weber's sociology, something he views as having basically served its term, reveals the differences between two conceptions of sociology and, more importantly, the ultimate choice between faith and hope and pessimism and tragedy.

1.   Shailer Mathews was born on 26th May 1863 in Maine and educated at Waterville College, Colby University, and finally Newton Theological Institution. After graduation he was appointed by Small as instructor in elocution at Colby and from 1890–92 took a sabbatical in Berlin. In 1894 he was appointed to a teaching position at Chicago, becoming professor successively of New Testament history (1897–1906), Historical and Comparative Theology (1906–26) and Historical Theology from 1926 until his retirement in 1933. He was dean of the Divinity School from 1908–33. He died in 1941. For a bibliography see Lindsay 1985.

2. *Shailer Mathews' Social Theology*

Shailer Mathews was raised in a climate where 'social problems, group morality, or economic life did not concern us' (Mathews 1936: 29). He did not know that 'there was a social order', only that 'God had been good to New England' (Mathews 1932: 164). Mathews first heard the word 'sociology' from Small (cf. Mathews 1936: 41) who, as president of Colby College, devoted almost all his energies to teaching a course on sociology, the third of its kind in the United States. After graduation he secured Mathews a post at Colby (cf. Smith and Sweet 1975), and it was again through his influence that Mathews moved to Chicago in 1894. They remained intimate friends until Small's death in 1926. However, it was a sabbatical in Berlin that finally led Mathews away from the restrictive evangelicalism of his childhood (Mathews 1924a: 10). Under Small's influence he studied not theology, but history, under Hans Delbrück, who encouraged 'the development of a critical sense and the impartial accumulation of data' (Mathews 1936: 42). Similarly, Delbrück's involvement in the *Evangelischer Sozial Kongress* (an institution which was also of vital importance in the development of Weber's sociology) helped to shape Mathews's recognition of the importance of sociology for the alleviation of social problems. Throughout his life Mathews kept up a rigorous regime of lecturing and of conducting retreats, thus never losing sight of the practical implications of his sociohistorical enterprise.

He eventually developed this into what he called 'Modernism' or 'the use of the methods of modern science to find, state and use the permanent and central values of inherited orthodoxy in meeting the needs of a modern world' (Mathews 1924a: 23). Such an 'evangelicalism of the scientific mind' which used 'modern methods to serve modern needs' set itself up against the 'evangelicalism of the dogmatic mind' (Mathews 1924a: 35-36), thus substituting the 'scientific method for reliance on authority'.[1] In biblical studies this grew into the sociohistorical method which by viewing biblical texts as products of their environment, helped to free them from their imprisonment in lower criticism.

---

1.   Mathews 1924b: 321. It is thus not surprising that Mathews should have become one of the leading foes of the fundamentalists. See especially Hynes 1981: 5ff.

Mathews' starting point was his view, which he shared with Small (Small 1916: 825), of human beings as gregarious by nature, who could only be understood 'as contributors to the action of the group of which they are members' (Mathews 1916: 21). The individual was conceived not as an 'isolated self-determining entity but a... portion of the total scheme of things, tied by a thousand threads to the encompassing whole' (Parrington 1933: 192). The distinctively modern problem, however, was that society, and particularly the alienating conditions of capitalism, threatened to overwhelm the individual altogether. 'Human life,' wrote Mathews, 'has passed from savagery, where that man was safest who was most alone, to the present chaos of relationships' (Mathews 1900: 456). What had to be sought was a balance or 'social unity' which would steer a course between a society which destroyed individuality and a complete separation of the individual from society. On Mathews' account, only religion could provide a basis for this fraternal ethic, since 'no people has ever become permanently unified on the basis of customs or civilisation' (Mathews 1900: 457).

Mathews' first major work bore the significant title 'Christian Sociology' (Mathews 1895–96, 1897–98), and was an exposition of 'the social philosophy and teachings of Christ' (Mathews 1895–96: 70) which provided the basis for all his subsequent work.[1] Although recognizing that obviously 'Jesus was not a student of society in the technical use of the term' (Mathews 1895–96: 77; cf. Mathews 1928: 43), Mathews held that a close look at his preaching revealed that 'no man's teaching has equalled his in the magnitude of its social results, and there are messages in his words yet to be heard... [The] sociologist who disregards the teachings of Christ is as unscientific as he who in the history of philosophy should neglect Plato and Kant' (Mathews 1895–96: 73).

Jesus' social teachings had, however, been all too often distorted by an evangelicalism where the 'new man and not a new society has been the objective point of most preaching' (Mathews 1895–96: 71) and where 'the belief in the triumph of a kingdom of love and righteousness has been replaced by expectation of joy in heaven or torture in hell' (Mathews 1928: 52). Against this '[we] need to be taught that

1. Although Mathews revised this essay (Mathews 1971) after the rediscovery of apocalyptic (see especially pp. 23ff.) his outline of Jesus' teaching survived almost unchanged.

religion is social as well as individualistic; that from the union of lives alone there can result safety and peace; and that the bundle into which lives are to be bound must be the life of God' (Mathews 1900: 469). This social dimension meant that asceticism was wholly absent from Jesus' teaching, which never made 'misery the thermometer of holiness' (Mathews 1897–98: 109). Instead, the 'member of the new society was not to flee the world, but was rather to stay in it as a source of light and life' (Mathews 1897–98: 110). The Christian ideal was 'not that of the monk but of the Christ' (Mathews 1897–98: 429) and 'goodness in the Christian sense' was 'social, not monastic' (Mathews 1899: 618). Thus 'a genuine Christianity makes men incapable of isolated life' (Mathews 1900: 457) and similarly 'a man cannot conform to the example of Jesus unless his life be joined consciously to others' (Mathews 1899: 617).

Jesus' social thought was naturally shaped by the social processes at work in the first century and made use of contemporary ideas, most importantly, the 'concrete, objective reality'[1] of the kingdom of God, which he saw as nothing less than 'an ideal (although progressively approximated) social order in which the relation of men to God is that of sons, and (therefore) to each other, that of brothers' (Mathews 1895–96: 367, 380). 'If each is a son of God,' Mathews asked, 'are they not brothers?' (Mathews 1897–98: 283; cf. Mathews 1900: 459).

The new order signified by the kingdom of God was marked by 'a universal reign of love—the fatherhood of God and the brotherhood of men' (Mathews 1895–96: 372), not in 'the limbo of utopia' (Mathews 1895–96: 377; cf. Mathews 1971: 63), but as progressively realizable in human life. Two elements were essential: '(1) the divine sonship as seen in the moral regeneration of the individual; and (2) the organic union of good men typified by the family' (Mathews 1895–96: 380; cf. Mathews 1971: 38-39). Although Mathews admitted that 'Jesus himself does not seem to use the parental analogy' nevertheless 'the fatherhood of God and the brotherhood of man' appeared to lie 'in the very heart of his teaching' (Mathews 1900: 460) and Jesus focused 'on the production of the socially minded individual dominated by goodwill' (Mathews 1971: 60). In this way, 'in his revelation of divine sonship and the consequent human brotherhood Jesus has

---

1.   In Mathews 1971, Mathews is far keener to emphasize the origin of Jesus' teaching in terms of the 'psychology of revolution' (p. 13). 'As a man of genius', however, Jesus never stepped across the 'limits of cold sanity' (pp. 36-37).

furnished the basis for lasting social progress' (Mathews 1897–98: 287). It was this principle of sonship and resultant fraternity, 'his elevation of love' (Mathews 1971: 52), that gave unity to the varied teachings of Jesus (Mathews 1897–98: 416).

After outlining this central or 'generic' principle of Jesus' teaching Mathews saw it as his overriding Christian duty 'to adjust the ideals of the past to conditions in the present' just as Jesus adjusted his teaching to the civilization of his own day.[1] In particular, there was a contemporary relevance to the idea of the kingdom of God which provided the basis for that 'evangelicalism that our age needs... [Let] men be reborn that, just because of their new natures which draw love from God himself, they may constitute a better social environment and a better humanity here on earth. In a word, through becoming sons, let Christians remember that they have become brothers' (Mathews 1899: 620).

For Mathews, social action was far more important than the metaphysical abstractions of theology (cf. Mathews 1900: 467). 'In a word,' Mathews said, 'religion breeds and disciplines *corporate enthusiasms*. Can the social movement afford to despise it?' (Mathews 1899: 620). He based this on Jesus himself who was far more concerned with 'passions and social trends... than with the intellect' (Mathews 1971: 40, 50). 'His real aim was practical—the preparation of men for the kingdom... He was not concerned with truth for truth's sake. He was not a philosopher but an organizer of a group on fire with radical hopes' (Mathews 1971: 45). Jesus contributed not 'a philosophy and a system... [but] a life and an attitude' (Mathews 1971: 147), which was to be reflected in a theology which had 'to be touched with social passion... to become a basis controlling social action' (Mathews 1971: 154). Similarly, the church had to become a 'lectureship, and, without puzzling men with strange theologies and stranger class sympathies, train them in the experience of Christian living' (Mathews 1900: 465; cf. Mathews 1971: 142). In this way '[the] prevention of tuberculosis and syphilis' became 'quite as much an element of duty as the maintenance of church-going' (Mathews 1971: 132). In short, 'social unity' was a 'fellowship in life, not in opinion' (Mathews 1900: 466).

Theology thus had to defer to sociology for the contemporary

---

1. Mathews 1971: 127. This later became the characteristic theme of his approach to church history. Cf. Mathews 1909: 24.

application of the fraternal ethic, which manifested itself in three distinctive ways.

1. Politics. Although Jesus gave no 'systematic teaching in regard to politics' (Mathews 1895–96: 609), 'one can no more call him an anarchist because he gives no political teaching than he can call him a surgeon because he never speaks of medicines' (Mathews 1895–96: 614). It was nevertheless possible to outline the direction of his thought which was based upon the fraternal ideal. Despite the inherent inequality of human beings, Jesus made a real call to fraternity, not as some other-worldly ideal or 'word for oratory and French public buildings' (Mathews 1897–98: 116), but as the 'enjoyment of love' (Mathews 1897–98: 116). This was expressed in the idea of the kingdom of God which was a 'union of brothers over whom God himself is to reign. Mankind is not composed of insulated individuals, but of social beings, who seek not a convenient association for exchange and other economic purposes, but an absorbing and organic union with one another as members of a family' (Mathews 1895–96: 615, 463). Consequently in any contemporary setting a 'government is Christian not because it is of this or that form, but because it is attempting to realize the principles of fraternity and love that underlie the entire social teachings of Jesus' (Mathews 1895–96: 617).

2. Economics. It was in the sphere of economics that Jesus spoke most often and 'with most emphasis' (Mathews 1895–96: 772), even though he 'had little interest in abstract questions' (Mathews 1895–96: 784). A Christian economics had to be founded on the truth that 'both manward and Godward a man is essentially a social being, and his life is imperfect in the same proportion as it is not in union with the life of others... For, like marriage, wealth concerns not the individual alone but society as well' (Mathews 1895–96: 778). Wealth was thus a good only when it was 'a social good' (Mathews 1895–96: 780).

3. Social order. Although Jesus taught fellowship (and on this minimum definition socialism was 'but a phase of Christianity' (Mathews 1895–96: 781)) it was nevertheless 'futile to attempt to discover modern socialism in the words of Jesus' (Mathews 1895–96: 782). The problem with the 'most important factors in the social awakening, socialism and sociology' was that they had been 'at least in the past... predominantly materialistic, and, if not aggressively atheistic, somewhat patronizing in their attitude toward the deity' (Mathews 1899: 605). Yet 'if there is anything unchristian', Mathews contended,

'it is the notion that bread and amusements and good drainage are going to bring in the millennium' (Mathews 1895–96: 783). We 'should challenge socialism to say why it arrogates to itself a monopoly of love for the masses, and challenge it again to say whether, instead of the Christian nation of kings and priests, its social regeneration through economic comfort will produce anything better than smug, selfish respectability' (Mathews 1899: 617). Against this Mathews held that '[no] social reform will be thoroughgoing and lasting that stops before endeavouring to bring every human being into the righteousness and fraternal love that springs from religious experience' (Mathews 1897–98: 428).

Thus in a social teaching loyal to Christ himself there was always an element of spiritual regeneration, which led to 'the change of a man's life from insulation to social union' (Mathews 1899: 618). The Christian picture of the world showed that human life was 'not under the sole control of economic forces' (Mathews 1971: 149); Jesus was 'the Son of Man, not the son of a class of men'. Nevertheless, 'his denunciation is unsparing of those men who make wealth at the expense of souls; who find in capital no incentive to further fraternity... for those men who are gaining the world but are letting their neighbour fall among thieves and Lazarus rot among their dogs' (Mathews 1895–96: 784). Socialism may not have been the only possible Christian teaching for Mathews, but its opposite seemed the very denial of fraternity itself.

Any contemporary realization of the generic principle of fraternity, which unified Jesus' teaching on politics, economics and social order, required a return to the 'normal life of men' revealed in the teaching of Christ that 'man is a social being' whose life was 'a twofold social relationship: a divine sonship and a human fraternity. These are the sources of the Christian motive that inevitably make toward the building up of both the individual and society' (Mathews 1897–98: 280; cf. Mathews 1895–96: 457, 1971: 67). Such reciprocal ideals, which had 'already rewrought civilizations as has no man or teaching', could help overcome the 'crisis in which the world is gripped' (Mathews 1897–98: 432) by leading human beings away from an 'atomistic, self-centred moral life' (Mathews 1897–98: 281; cf. Mathews 1971: 152) to a 'new sonship'. This 'would result in new moral impulses' (Mathews 1897–98: 281) embodied in 'a multitude of fraternal loves which, disregarding place, and time, and birth, and social station, will forever remain unsatisfied until they express themselves in reciprocal deeds of kindness and bring in a new social order' (Mathews 1897–98: 284). In the end this would lead to the 'triumph of this new and perfected humanity... [to] the coming of the Lord' (Mathews 1897–98: 431).

Finally, Mathews asked whether this noble principle of fraternity was realizable. Did people 'really believe that it is possible to organize society on the principles of Jesus?' (Mathews 1971: 154). His answer was unequivocal. The return to the normal human condition of fraternity would be gradual, not *en masse* but as each individual realized its 'fraternal love' (Mathews 1897–98: 423). Although Jesus taught fraternity, he 'was never so crude a thinker as to imagine that society is a mechanical mixture of elements into which it must be disintegrated as a step towards a happier recombination. With him progress was biological, an evolution rather than a revolution' (Mathews 1897–98: 113). Thus, Mathews held, 'the expanding Christian society... will consist of groups of individuals each possessed of the same spirit and method of life as that taught by their Master' (Mathews 1897–98: 424-25; cf. Mathews 1971: 55). In short, 'the test of a theory or a program must not be, does Jesus teach it? but does it make for fraternity?' (Mathews 1971: 113).

Ultimately, according to Mathews, society could be transformed only through an individual repentance which would gradually lead to social regeneration: 'to make men Christians is to make society unified' (Mathews 1900: 461; cf. Mathews 1897–98: 422). Only personal regeneration could allow for the survival of individuality in the face of the overwhelming threats of society. Against this, 'the statistical study of social groups and the attempt to legislate men out of their vices' were little more than 'expressions of a sense of impotence of the individual in the midst of social forces' (Mathews 1971: 150). With Jesus, however, there was 'freedom and hope for men however socially submerged or economically dependent' (Mathews 1971: 150). The whole direction of Mathews's thought moves towards a reciprocal fraternal relationship between regenerate individuals:

> A person dominated by the faith and hope of Jesus has been reborn into spiritual unity. Dissociated motives and localized habits have been replaced by a dominant attitude or mind-set toward the ideal of a social good. The significant fact, however, is that this ideal of Jesus is not

abstract but concrete. Jesus thus makes prominent social rather than meta-physical goals. Neither the state nor society, abstract goodness nor duty, but a more personal because more social individual, is the end of the quest for perfection. His teaching as love, expressed in other words, means that social relations are functional, serving the progress of spiritual and per-sonal values of the individual (Mathews 1971: 152).

Religion alone provided the individual with a spiritual unity which would act as a guide through the narrow straits between the oppres-sion of materialism and the ethical indifference of individualism.

3. *The Principle of Fraternity in Max Weber*

The alternative is expressed by Max Weber who, writing in a very different context, saw no future for the fraternal ethic of the Christian religion as an all-embracing socially unifying principle since it was hopelessly out of touch with the modern world. This is perhaps most succinctly stated in his incisive response to Gertrud Bäumer of 1916. The power of the Gospels to speak directly to the present had been rendered null and void not merely by world war but by the modern world itself. Indeed the purest of ethical motives could have the most destructive results:

> [The Gospels] stand in contradiction not just to war—which they do not especially single out—but ultimately to each and every law of the social world in so far as these involve a world of culture which is centred on the here and now, that is on beauty, value, honour and the greatness of the 'creature'. . . It is only within this system of laws that the current 'demands of the day' have any relevance. . . The old sober empiricist J.S. Mill said: 'empiricism alone will never arrive at the idea of *one* God—at least, in my opinion, at the God of goodness, but at a *polythe-ism*. In fact whoever is in the world (in a Christian sense) can never experience anything but a conflict between a plethora of values. . . He has to *choose* when to serve one God and when another'.[1]

The theme of polytheism recurs in 1918. Science, Weber held, could not reveal absolutes: it could never answer the question, 'Which of the warring Gods are we to serve?' (Weber 1948a: 153).

Similarly, in discussing the vocation of politics, Weber held that the human being could no longer choose between conflicting values solely

---

1. Weber 1971: 145. All translations are my own. On Weber's relation to the German theology of his time, see Chapman 1993.

on the basis of the Sermon on the Mount. Ethical absolutes, including fraternity, had served their term. If the historical and political realities of the contemporary world were brought into consideration, the choice rested between the greater and lesser evil, since 'the genius, or the demon of politics, lives in an inward tension with the God of love' (Weber 1948b: 126). By refusing to resist evil with force, for instance, politicians made themselves responsible for the increase of evil which resulted from inaction (cf. Weber 1948b: 120). Consequently the absolutist ethics of fraternity could have little role within the 'ethical irrationality of the world' (Weber 1948b: 122). The mark of political maturity was thus the knowledge or the understanding of the immutable conditions of life and thus, although Weber recognized that absolutist ethics provided the ultimate *motivation* for action, it was only possible to construct a coherent system for social and political action if all the consequences of behaviour were taken into account since social and historical reality or 'factuality' tempered all ethical activity. 'A successful politics,' Weber remarked, 'is the "art of the possible"', even if 'it is no less true that the possible is often reached only by striving to the impossible that lies beyond it' (Weber 1973: 51).

There was, however, a point at which the conflict between absolutist ethics ('the impossible') and political reality ('the possible') reached a 'unison' which forced the mature individual to assert, in Luther's terms, 'Here I stand, I can do no other' (Weber 1948b: 127). Yet for Weber such a stand, which was reserved for heroic leaders, would lead to a political sociology far removed from Mathews' 'Christian Sociology' where, in Christian fraternity, all people were equally sons and daughters of God. For Weber, political maturity was a gift for the few who could responsibly use power within the hostile and immutable confines of factuality, whereas for Mathews, it was a divine gift—the gift of sonship and fraternity conferred on all for the benefit of all and for the sake of a transformation of factuality itself.

4. Conclusions: Heroes or Brothers

In the end Mathews retained a ray of hope that the principle of fraternity as an expression of personal and social regeneration, which he had found at the centre of the Synoptic Gospels, would provide a satisfactory basis, when combined with modern statistical research, to transform society into the kingdom of God. Such transformation did not require the tragic heroes of Weber's divine comedy, but the power conferred by the simple acceptance of the love of God as the

> practicable basis upon which to build human relations. Once let humanity actually believe this and the perspective of values will be changed. Giving justice will replace fighting for rights; the democratizing of privilege will replace the manipulation of social advantages; the humanizing of necessary economic processes will replace the exploiting of human life in the interests of wealth or pleasure (Mathews 1971: 155).

Such principles, although usually less consciously voiced, similarly provided the motivating force for most of the early Chicago sociologists. Mathews' attempt to justify the principle of social individuality on the basis of the New Testament tradition, without thereby glorifying individualism or submerging individuality in the sea of social forces, forms a powerful reminder of the need to look at the ethical principles undergirding any sociology which claims to be anything more than descriptive. Mathews and his American contemporaries in sociology were well aware that a prescriptive sociology works with an ethical end in sight, and also that this end had all too often been misunderstood or inadequately discussed. Although his historical method might now seem hopelessly dated he nevertheless worked with a clear perception of a goal which would form the point of orientation for all social transformations of the present. Such a goal, which he summarized as the principle of fraternity, he saw as emerging in Scripture and as upheld through the Christian tradition.

The answer which Mathews would have given to Weber's question, 'Which of the warring Gods are we to serve?', is clear. He opted for the God who preached co-operation between human beings, thereby sharing the faith and hope in a better future which inspired the University of Chicago in its early days. In contrast to the Nietzschean pessimism of Weberian polytheism, Mathews maintained a faith in the triumph of love, not by cataclysm or by Caesarist leadership, but by social progress. For him it was clear that 'the evidence that the "will to love" is superior to the "will to power" lies in the very nature of our world' (Mathews 1971: 54). Tragically, however, as Weber observed, such evidence depended far more on faith than nature. In the end sociology conceived as social progress *needs* religion.

We can conclude only by asking a set of questions. Can the ideal of fraternity survive as the basis for social regeneration? Or is it no longer a realizable ideal in a world where the individual has been divorced from all social expressions of individuality? Is there a future for the hope of rational and progressive social amelioration against the pessimism of the rampant and oppressive factuality, the 'iron cage', of Weberian reality? And if the foundations for fraternity as the guiding principle of social transformation can no longer depend on a sacred text, as they did for Mathews, then where are they to be located? Indeed, if there is to be a survival of fraternity, and its universalistic expression in the Enlightenment ideal of humanity, can it rest on any basis other than faith?

For Weber, as for the theologian Rudolf Bultmann (Bultmann 1969: 44), the Sermon on the Mount was hopelessly alien to the contemporary world. Yet, for Mathews and Small, there was always a hope that the ideal of fraternity might gain a foothold in concrete history, something which, in the words of their contemporary Ernst Troeltsch, required 'a position towards the world and towards life which rests on faith' (Troeltsch 1991: 233). The ultimate choice between Mathews and Weber admittedly rests with the individual's decision, but the alternative to a faith in something at least resembling the biblical principle of fraternity, however demythologized, as a realizable ideal, is frankly grotesque, to which the parody of fraternity preached by a more recent Chicago School (of economics) bears witness. There is always the grave danger that in a world no longer capable of expressing fraternity, another biblical myth will take its place and 'the tower of Babel,' as Troeltsch wrote, 'might become a symbol of a European kingdom of the giants which has neglected God. *Deus afflavit et dissipati sunt'*—God blew and they were scattered (Troeltsch 1991: 234). Fraternity, on the other hand, demands a different myth—not giants and heroes, but sons and daughters of God.

References

Ames, E.S.
  1959   *Beyond Theology* (Chicago).
Barnes, H.E.
  1948   'Albion Woodbury Small', in *An Introduction to the History of Sociology* (Chicago).
Bulmer, M.
  1984   *The Chicago School of Sociology: Institutionalization, Diversity and the Rise of Sociological Research* (Chicago).

Bultmann, R.
  1969 [1964]   'Liberal Theology and the Latest Theological Movement', in *Faith and Understanding*, I (ed. R.W. Funk, trans. L.P. Smith; London). Originally published in German as 'Die liberale Theologie und die jüngste theologische Bewegung', in *Glaube und Verstehen*, I (Tübingen, 1964).
Chapman, M.D.
  1993   'Polytheism and Personality', in *History of the Human Sciences*, 6.
Dibble, V.
  1975   *The Legacy of Albion Small* (Chicago).
Faris, R.E.L.
  1970   *Chicago Sociology, 1920–1932* (Chicago).
Hinkle, R.C., and G.J. Hinkle
  1954   *The Development of Modern Sociology: Its Nature and Growth in the United States* (New York).
Hynes, W.J.
  1981   *Shirley Jackson Case and the Chicago School: The Socio-Historical Method* (Chico, CA).
Hofstadter, R.
  1955   *The Age of Reform* (New York).
Lindsay, W.D.
  1985   'Shailer Mathews: A Comprehensive Bibliography', *American Journal of Theology and Philosophy* 6, pp. 3-27.
Mathews, S.
  1895–96   'Christian Sociology' (Part I), *American Journal of Sociology* 1 (later published with Mathews 1897–98 as *The Social Teachings of Jesus* [New York, 1897]).
  1897–98   'Christian Sociology' (Part II), *American Journal of Sociology* 2.
  1899   'The Church and the Social Movement', *American Journal of Sociology* 4.
  1900   'The Christian Church and Social Unity', *American Journal of Sociology* 5.
  1909   'A Positive Method for an Evangelical Theology', *American Journal of Sociology* 13.
  1916   'The Historical Study of Religion', in G.B. Smith (ed.), *A Guide to the Study of the Christian Religion* (Chicago).
  1924a   *The Faith of Modernism* (Chicago).
  1924b   *The Contributions of Science of Religion* (New York).
  1971 [1928]   *Jesus on Social Institutions* (Philadelphia).
  1932   'Theology as Group Belief', in V. Ferm (ed.), *Contemporary American Theology*, II (New York).
  1936   *New Faith for Old* (New York).
Parrington, V.
  1933   *Main Currents in American Thought: Beginnings of Critical Realism in America, 1860–1920*, III (New York).
Small, A.
  1895   'The Era of Sociology', *American Journal of Sociology* 1.
  1907   *Adam Smith and Modern Sociology* (Chicago).
  1910   *The Meaning of Social Science* (Chicago).

1916 'Fifty Years of Sociology in the United States', *American Journal of Sociology* 21.

Smith, K., and L. Sweet
1975 'Shailer Mathews: A Chapter in the Social Gospel Movement', *Foundations* 17.

Troeltsch, E.
1991 [1922] *Religion in History* (Edinburgh). Originally published in German, *Die Sozialphilosophie des Christentums* (Zürich, 1922).

Weber, M.
1948a 'Science as a Vocation', in *From Max Weber: Essays on Sociology* (ed. and trans. H.H. Gerth and C. Wright Mills; London). German edition, 'Wissenschaft als Beruf', in J. Winckelmann (ed.), *Gesammelte Aufsätze zur Wissenschaftslehre* (Tübingen, 1973).

1948b 'Politics as a Vocation', in *From Max Weber: Essays on Sociology* (ed. and trans. H.H. Gerth and C. Wright Mills; London). German edition, 'Politik als Beruf', in J. Winckelmann (ed.), *Gesammelte Politische Schriften* (Tübingen, 1971).

1971 'Zwischen zwei Gesetzen', in J. Winckelmann (ed.), *Gesammelte Politische Schriften* (Tübingen).

1973 'Der Sinn der "Wertfreiheit"', in J. Winckelmann (ed.), *Gesammelte Aufsätze zur Wissenschaftslehre* (Tübingen).

The Quaker *Book of Discipline*:
A Sacred Text by Committee?

Kathleen Thomas

The subtitle of this paper is not entirely facetious. It was in 1988 that I heard a new edition of the Quaker *Book of Discipline* was being prepared. A few weeks ago when I enquired whether it was now ready, a Quaker friend replied, 'Oh no! it will be some time yet—after all it is being done by committee'.

So what exactly is this book? The edition now in use consists of two parts. The first volume is entitled *Christian Faith and Practice in the Experience of the Society of Friends* and was printed in 1960; the second volume, entitled *Church Government*, appeared in 1968.[1]

The first part, after a brief introduction and three epigraphic quotations consists of fifteen chapters. The first comprises 115 extracts, including four poems, from the writings of individual Quakers, ranging from the seventeenth century, with entries from the works of George Fox and William Penn, through the eighteenth and nineteenth to the mid-twentieth with entries from John Woolman, Elizabeth Fry and John Bright—to name just a few of the Quakers known far outside the Society. These excerpts tell of the spiritual experiences and insights gained by these people during their lives, whether as itinerant preacher or missionary, as reformer or politician, as teacher, banker, businessman, relief worker or doctor. Each quotation is preceded by a short biographical note on the author, setting the context in which it was written.

The next six chapters also consist of quotations on such subjects as

1. *Book of Christian Discipline of the London Yearly Meeting of the Religious Society of Friends*. I. *Christian Faith and Practice in the Society of Friends* (London: Friends Book Centre, repr., 1972 [1959]; II. *Church Government* (London: Friends Book Centre, repr., 1980).

'Christian experience and the formulation of belief', 'God as Creator and Father', 'Science and Religion', 'The Person and Work of Christ', 'The Scriptures', 'Creeds', 'Sacraments', 'Friends and other Faiths', 'Corporate Worship', Vocal Ministry', 'Retirement and Prayer'. The excerpts here and in the remainder of the book, in addition to many from individuals, include extracts from the Minutes of the Yearly Meetings and from the Epistles sent out to Quaker Meetings throughout the country giving advice and encouragement. Sometimes passages are taken from reports of national or international conferences.

The last chapters deal rather with the practice of Quakerism—membership, the caring fellowship, the officers, marriage, careers, education, social, national and international responsibilities, together with practical advice on the making of wills, teaching science, enjoying the arts, the promotion of health and the treatment of animals. The final chapter describes, still in the form of quotations, the world family of Friends.

Volume II, *Church Government*, begins with a brief history of the *Advices and Queries* which are addressed to each constituent Meeting[1] of the Society or each individual member. Then come the *Advices*, some five pages, followed by 23 *Queries*, together with a reminder of the duty of reading these.

Chapters 17–29 deal with church affairs, the structure and conduct of business meetings, Standing Committees, duties of the Clerk, Elders and Overseers, marriage regulations, ordering of burials and cremations, and lastly finance.

The preamble to the last, thirtieth, chapter includes these words: 'This final chapter gives a few portraits of Friends, that we may remind ourselves that our *Church Government* is not an abstract code of regulations but the embodiment of the Society's experience'. Seven 'Portraits' follow, portraits of very different personalities. The whole is rounded off with a reminder that Friends work always as instruments of God.

The sentence just quoted states that the *Book of Discipline* is the product of a society's experience: indeed, it is an experience gathered

1.   'Meeting' with an upper-case 'M' refers to a unit of the organization of the Society of Friends. Quarterly Meetings no longer exist. At present there are Preparative Meetings (for the local worshipping group), Monthly Meetings (area group) and Yearly Meetings (for example the London Yearly Meeting is for the whole of the UK).

over three centuries. It is now in its seventh edition, the first having been printed in the late eighteenth century: but the history of its production does not start there.

As already pointed out, some of the passages are taken from Epistles. The first Epistle was issued in 1656 by a general meeting called at Balby in Yorkshire.[1] The date is important. There had been smaller general meetings in the preceding four years, where matters of importance to the growing movement were discussed. In October 1656, however, an event took place which greatly disturbed all Quakers: James Nayler, a leader of the movement together with Fox, rode into Bristol on a donkey accompanied by women waving branches and crying 'hosanna'. Nayler declared that he had done this as a sign that Christ had come and was really present in people's hearts. The civil authorities, however, regarded it as blasphemous and condemned him to brutal punishment followed by imprisonment.[2] The incident and its result naturally caused alarm in the whole Quaker community, and it is clear that the Balby meeting and the Epistle were brought about by the social circumstances, that is intensified threats and actual persecution by legal means. This Epistle contains instructions to all Friends on attendance at meetings, vocal ministry, the treatment of disorderly walkers, arrangement and recording of marriages and burials, the care of the poor, of widows and servants, of prisoners and their families, appearance before the courts, public service, honesty in trading and guarding against malicious gossip and being busybodies. Some of these provisions were essential since the members accepted none of the ministrations of the established church nor parish relief. Copies of the Epistle were then taken to the groups in the surrounding area. The provisions do read as instructions, but a postscript was added which makes clear the Quaker position that the leading of the Spirit in each member is the real source of guidance:

> Dearly beloved Friends, these things we do not lay upon you as a rule or form to walk by, but that all, with the measure of light which is pure and

---

1. See W.C. Braithwaite, *The Beginnings of Quakerism* (London: Macmillan, 1912), pp. 310-13.

2. See E. Fogelklou, *James Nayler, The Rebel Saint* (trans. Yapp; London: Benn, 1931).

holy, may be guided: and so in the light walking and abiding, these things
may be fulfilled in the Spirit, not from the letter, for the letter killeth, but
the Spirit giveth life.

Similar general meetings were called in the years following in various parts of the country and Epistles issued. All these letters were
composed by groups of leaders—'weighty friends', as they were
called—with a view to providing protective guidance and encouragement to the relatively isolated groups. They played a part in welding
the diffuse movement together. From 1681 onwards a general meeting
for the whole country was held annually in London and an Epistle
issued after each.

In 1738 the Yorkshire Quarterly Meeting requested that a digest be
made of the most important parts of the Epistles and Minutes already
issued. Excerpts were selected and written in a folio volume, which
was circulated in manuscript. One of these was sold to each Quarterly
Meeting for fifty shillings—a quite considerable sum in those days.
These volumes were known as *The Book of Extracts*. The topics in
this book were arranged in alphabetical order, beginning with Appeals
and Arbitrations through Fighting, Kings and Governors, Law, Love,
Marriage and Meeting Houses to Negroes, Oaths, Orphans,
Parliament, Scripture, Singing, and ending with Tithes, Trading and
Tombstones. A handy book of reference for dealing with life's
problems!

The section headed 'Advices and Queries' in the current edition, and
in many of its predecessors, has a slightly different history. In 1682
the London Yearly Meeting decided to put three questions to the representatives of the Quarterly Meetings to elicit information on the
state of the Society. These asked how many Ministers[1] had died, what
Friends had died in prison, and how Truth had prospered, that is to
say, had the Meeting expanded, during the last year. Oral replies were
to be given. Over the years the number of questions increased, written
replies replaced oral ones, and in 1723 the term 'query' was substituted for 'question'. Recommendations and counsels were also sent out
as occasion demanded and these became known as 'advices'.

The first *Book of Discipline* to be printed appeared in 1783 and was

---

1.   A Quaker Minister was a member who was considered fit to speak at
meetings and to travel on behalf of the Society as a preacher. They were recorded
until 1924.

entitled 'Extracts from the Minutes and Advices'. At first no individual was allowed to possess a copy, but each Monthly Meeting was expected to have one for the guidance of those in authority—the Elders and Ministers. Quakerism had developed into a sect and the accumulated wisdom was in the hands of an elite. Since answers to the queries were required—and the phrasing of the question indicated what the answer should be—the book had become a means of social control.

In the early nineteenth century the Enlightenment and the Evangelical revival had an impact on the Society of Friends, causing a major split in America and minor divergences in England. The Yearly Meeting decided at this point to insert statements of doctrine into the *Book of Discipline*. The first was a letter from Fox to the Governor of Barbados in 1671.[1] This reads like a much expanded version of the Nicene Creed, with extra paragraphs on the Scriptures and on instructing families, including Negroes and Indians, in the faith. It was clearly written to ease the path of the Quaker missionaries, for Fox's *Journal* at all times shows that the main thrust of his message concerned the Divine Light in everyone, including unconverted Indians, and the primacy of this inward light over creeds and scriptures.

However, this letter was seized on by those influenced by the evangelical movement and by those who saw such a declaration as a protection against deism. It was inserted into the *Book of Discipline*— along with a statement of faith[2] by a Meeting of 1693 when a division was threatened in the British Society. This second statement was amply supplied with biblical references.

These two statements together formed the chapter on 'Doctrine', the first part of the 1834 edition, which was now called *Rules of Discipline* and no longer had the subjects arranged in alphabetical order. It would not be true to say that the development of Quakerism fitted neatly into the usual progression of movement to sect to denomination, but during the eighteenth and the first half of the nineteenth centuries it certainly exhibited the common characteristics of a sect. These characteristics are reflected both in the title and the content of the *Book*. It was partly as an answer to the decline in numbers in the

1. G. Fox, *Journal* (ed. J.L. Nickalls; London: Religious Society of Friends, 1952), pp. 602-606.
2. See W.C. Braithwaite, *The Second Period of Quakerism* (London: Macmillan, 1919), pp. 378, 495.

mid-eighteenth century that the discipline was tightened. The number of queries was increased to twenty, many now enquiring into private prayer, personal witness and attendance at meetings. Light in the individual was felt to be in need of control by the leading 'weighty Friends'.

In the second half of the nineteenth century some Friends began to realize that it might actually have been the rigid discipline which had led to a reduction in numbers. This resulted in a relaxation of various rules: members were no longer to be 'disowned', that is expelled, for marrying outside the Society, censorship was abolished, and the peculiarities of dress became optional. The title of the 1883 edition was changed to the *Book of Christian Discipline* and was given a long subtitle about its being extracts. The statements of faith still appear in the first section on doctrine, but they have been shortened and passages from later Epistles, dated after 1852, are added which, though still speaking of doctrine, place more emphasis on life in the Spirit.

It was not until the early twentieth century that a major change was made in the *Book of Discipline*, one which reflected seventy years of slow liberalization of the Society. The years around the turn of the century saw a flourishing of interest in the history of the Society, in the tenets and witness of its founding members. This led to a deeper and broader understanding of the activity of the Divine Light. Friends now saw that all previous versions of their Book lacked the testimony to personal experience of the living Spirit, which in the eyes of the founder was the real source of authority, and is considered so today. Each of the three editions of the nineteenth century was printed in one volume. The first section had been devoted to Doctrine, but in 1921 this appeared as a separate volume called *Christian Life, Faith and Thought in the Society of Friends*. This part consists of excerpts from the writings of thirty-four different Quakers, beginning with passages from Fox's *Journal* and ending with a poem by Thomas Hodgkin written in 1913. These excerpts, together with short biographical notes, are the basis of the first chapter of the current edition. The previous lack of Friends' personal experience has been amply compensated for. There follow some doctrinal statements, but the editors assert that, 'to us creeds have no value save as they testify to the eternal realities which men must apprehend by spiritual experience and express in life and conduct. A vital creed is not static but dynamic'. They continue: 'Thus while truth is eternal, our apprehension of it enlarges, and our expression of it changes, and Friends do not feel prepared to pin their adhesion to a form of words which at best embody a sincere attempt to define that measure of truth which has so far been apprehended in words appropriate to the age in which they are spoken'.[1]

The rest of the *Book of Discipline* was printed in two more volumes, *Christian Practice* and *Church Government*, which appeared in 1925 and 1931 respectively. The introductory remarks emphasize that all three volumes are to be regarded as one book, for 'the way of life is inseparable from its inspiration'. Most of the passages in these two last volumes are from Epistles, Minutes and Reports of Conferences and Committees.

The current edition, the seventh, presents *Christian Faith and Practice* together in one volume. The number of excerpts from individual Quakers is considerably increased, including passages from the Swarthmore[2] lectures by leading personalities such as Arthur Eddington and Russell Brain. The choice of passages is wide-ranging, both in date and subject matter. It is noticeable that, in both these editions, the proportion of items from men to those from women is approximately three to one. Women members have always outnumbered men, though at present the ratio of the sexes in the Society is nearly fifty-fifty. Women have always been considered equal in meetings for worship though they did not receive full equality in business meetings until 1896. Fewer women have recorded their spiritual experiences—and the choice has been made mainly by men.

In 1968 the 'Advices' included recommendations on the right use of radio and television, and the 'Queries' were brought up to date by additional questions regarding the wise use of man's power over nature, and the necessity of exercising brotherly love irrespective of race, and of examining the causes of social injustice. 'Advices' and 'Queries' both emphasize a willingness to subject every part of life towards communion with God and with one's fellow creatures. It is at

1. *Christian Life, Faith and Thought in the Society of Friends* (1921), pp. 64-65.
2. The Swarthmore Lectureship was established by the Woodbrooke Extension Committee in 1907 and involves 'an annual lecture on some subject relating to the message and work of the Society of Friends'. The name was chosen in memory of the home of Margaret Fox. It is delivered on the evening preceding the Friends Yearly Meeting in each year, for members and for the wider public. Since 1966 each lecture has been published by the Friends Home Service Committee.

the end of these exhortations that we now find quoted the postscript to the first ever Epistle, that from Balby in 1656.

Thus the Quaker *Book of Discipline* has developed over three hundred years, new editions having appeared at twenty- to thirty-year intervals. Not only words but life-style and practical arrangements are to be appropriate to the age. One of Fox's reasons for abandoning the sacraments was because they were not appropriate to the age of the Spirit. The excerpts in all editions are dated, and the preface to the 1921 edition explicitly directs that 'careful attention should be paid to the dates of the different documents and extracts'. Attitudes and emphases changed even during the early days in the seventeenth century, and have continued to do so. Change in the 'sacred text' has been gradual—Fox's statement on doctrine, not introduced until the evangelical period, was first abbreviated before being discarded altogether. The 'canon', we might say, is neither final nor irrevocable. What sort of society produced—and continues to produce—such a sacred text? It is one where life experience is valued as the source of understanding. It may be that of a singular individual: then one set of experiences is put side by side with others which offer a slightly different view or insight. A representative social group selects the passages they think most inspiring for inclusion. If the passage is from a report or Epistle, then we must remember how minutes and official reports are made in Friends' Meetings: each minute is composed by the Clerk who judges the 'sense of the Meeting', writes the minute, and then reads it aloud to obtain the approval of all present. The written report expresses consensus—all must agree or the discussion continues and the minute is rewritten.[1] The Quaker *Book of Discipline* is the fruit of the dynamic between the personal and the corporate, between the insights of charismatic leaders and the collective wisdom of a social group. The method of production seems to bear some resemblance to the 'corporate writing' indulged in at present by a group of Anglican scholars and bishops preparing a document on the Holy Spirit; but this is unlikely to be treated as a sacred text!

Is the Quaker *Book of Discipline* in fact treated as a sacred text? What use is made of it? The first *Book of Extracts* was requested by a general meeting so that the scattered groups throughout the country could refer to the accumulated wisdom of the Society and thus gain

---

1.   For an independent observer's account see M. Sheeran SJ, *Beyond Majority Rule* (Philadelphia: Philadelphia Yearly Meeting, 1983).

help in dealing with day-to-day concerns. For a time, as we have seen, only the Elders were given access to the book: those in high standing locally used the book to dispense wisdom to the rest of the members. Later explicit instructions were given about the use of the 'Advices' and 'Queries'. In the 1883 edition it is directed that the advices are to be read once a year at the close of a meeting for worship, so that not only members but also attenders will hear them. They are to be read in Quarterly, Monthly, and Women's and Men's Meetings for Discipline. The queries are also to be read and 'seriously considered' at least once a year, separately and periodically as the local meetings think fit. A few queries requiring information about the meetings are to be answered by the meetings as a group. The other queries are to be used by every friend 'to examine whether he himself is coming up in that life of self-denial and devotedness to God which so highly becomes all who make profession of the name of Christ'. A formula is thus set for self-examination leading to silent confession and reform of life. Is this a substitute for auricular confession? The reading of the book may cause a metaphorical rending of garments leading to a return to the principles of the readers' forbears, in a way reminiscent of the result of King Josiah's discovery and reading of the Book of the Law.

In 1931 the directions for use were less definite: both advices and queries 'are to be kept before the members of our Religious Society'. They are to be read in Quarterly Meetings and in addition 'one or more may be read from time to time' 'most suitably in a meeting for worship'. In 1968 it was simply stated that 'the Advices and Queries are intended for use in our Meetings and for private devotion'. The only duty is to send a report of the use made. Such phrases as 'generally it will be helpful to arrange' or 'Friends may wish to consider' set the tone of the book.

A small part of the new *Book of Discipline* now being compiled is entitled 'Questions and Counsel'—an updating of language—and has already been produced. At the Newcastle Meeting each Elder has the book for a month, during which time he or she may read part in a meeting for worship, but only 'if moved to do so'. The leadings of the Spirit are paramount. In practice, I am told, the Spirit frequently does not so move. There is also no insistence that the new form must be read—the old is still acceptable. There is surely some similarity with the use of different translations of the Bible or the 1662 *Book of*

Common Prayer and *Alternative Service Book* in Anglican worship today. In the Quaker book there is a gradual lessening of rigour in the recommendations for use.

One further significant use is made of the *Book of Discipline*. Each newly convinced person is given a copy inscribed by the Clerk of the Meeting as a sign of his or her acceptance as a member of the Society. A book which a community has produced by accumulation and selection over the years is now used as a sign of bonding. The current *Book of Discipline* has, in all, 998 entries, excluding the editorial notes. These entries range from the description of a mystical experience to the precise wording of a certificate of marriage, from an account of the Boston Martyrs to the duties of Elders, from factual details to a devotional poem. This might strike one as a hotchpotch— but how much does it differ from the Hebrew Scriptures? They too include precise instructions for worship and for daily life, historical accounts, prophetic utterances and poems.

Again, just as the Hebrew Scriptures express what it is to be a Jew, so the *Book of Discipline* expresses what it is to be a Quaker. The reader learns that 'these are the sort of experiences Quakers have', 'these are the people whose memory we honour', 'these are the life-styles we strive to adopt', 'these are the ways we deal with everyday matters', 'this is the way we organize our community'. The member of the Society is provided with an identity. A special environment is created in which a member finds his or her place and knows who he or she is. It is primary knowledge not theoretical legitimation.

The early leaders of the Quaker movement are said to have known the Christian Bible, both the Old and the New Testaments, almost by heart. Their own writings show intimate familiarity with the exact words. In the Quaker view, however, Scripture was, and is, secondary to the leadings of the Spirit, the Spirit which 'will lead into all truth'. Excerpts once considered suitable for inclusion may at a later date be excluded. The lasting impression made by the Quaker sacred text is that, while retaining the best and most profound insights of the movement's founders and successors, it is still developing and changing as the Society interprets its basic message for each succeeding generation. The expectation is that it will continue to change and develop, for the Quakers' fundamental principle is that the Spirit is alive in everyone and will guide to fresh understandings of the mystery of life. The title of the *Book of Discipline* may give the wrong impression to an outsider. Perhaps we should think of it as a 'Book of Discipleship'—a book recording the experiences of those on the way of spiritual enlightenment and directing attention to the sources of inspiration and proven ways of bearing witness.

Part 4: Women

Introduction to Part 4: Women

Jon Davies and Isabel Wollaston

Few would disagree with the claim that gender (like class, race, ethnicity and sexual orientation) is one of the determinants that shape an individual's life. Yet, having stated what seems to be the obvious, we feel compelled to agree with Gerda Lerner when she points out that the experience and insights of women are all too often 'missing' from history and theology, as those subjects have traditionally been articulated, studied and taught. Women are also either 'missing' or marginal in the majority of the sacred texts of the world's great religions. The two papers in this section explore, albeit in very different ways, the response of women to this situation. In effect, they document the struggle of women to 'become visible', and to have their say in naming both the world and the sacred.

In considering the case of women in southern Nigeria, Rosalind Hackett shows how women live in a world defined and generally dominated by men, yet still succeed in shaping and influencing the religious life of their communities. She documents the emergence of a number of different, mainly Pentecostalist, groups devoted to exploring the specific concerns of women and developing a distinctively female religiosity. Her thesis is that the Bible is used to legitimate women's assumption of an increasingly active and influential role in the leadership and spiritual direction of religious communities, while also serving to perpetuate the status quo. Hackett suggests that women in Nigeria are indeed attaining spiritual equality, but in a way which retains and indeed reinforces their domestic inequality.

While Hackett documents women's struggle to live within an existing framework and adapt it to their particular needs, Linda Anderson considers the attempt of one writer—Toni Morrison—to articulate an alternative definition of the sacred, one arising out of and speaking to the experience of black women in America. The implication of Anderson's paper is that women are developing an alternative 'canon' of sacred texts, which will either displace or remain in uneasy coexistence with the traditional canon. These alternative sacred texts explore the absences and silences in recorded history, highlighting the significance of what has been unwritten and unremembered. Morrison's novel, *Beloved*, highlights the fact that it is not only the experience of women that has been excluded from history: the same applies to the experience of slaves and, to a large extent, the black community in America. Anderson concludes her paper by appealing for a definition of the sacred which is both more all-embracing and more threatening than is conventional. She suggests that rather than being understood as mystification or idealization, the sacred should be identified with the attempt to speak the unspeakable, with the liminal space of risk and terror. Encountering the sacred is fraught with danger: it is an encounter with the repressed and forgotten meanings of history, with those experiences which resist expression.

Anderson and Hackett are both concerned with the articulation of vernacular understandings of the sacred. As with the papers on prayer in Part 2, they highlight the continued existence and subversive effect of alternatives to 'official' theologies and understandings of history and our relation to the sacred.

From Exclusion to Inclusion:
Women and Bible Use in Southern Nigeria

Rosalind I.J. Hackett

From the earliest stages of Christianity in Nigeria, the Bible was viewed as the key to Western power and technological and commercial success. In Old Calabar, for example, in southeastern Nigeria (where the Scottish Presbyterians first established their mission in 1846), letters sent by the chiefs to Queen Victoria requesting missionaries attest to this perception of 'God-man's fashion'—'Mr Blyth tell me England glad for send man to teach book and teach for understand God all same as whiteman'.[1] On reception of the large Bibles brought by the incoming missionaries in 1846, King Eyo Honesty II is reported to have said, 'Now I am sure God will love and bless me, for I am glad you come with this book'.[2]

Missionary teachings placed the Bible at the heart of commerce and civilization. This linking of sacred knowledge and 'secular' prosperity was readily accepted in the Nigerian context, although such knowledge was considered the privilege of a male (initiated) elite.[3] In this regard the education of the female population met with strong cultural opposition in the early days of the mission: 'They can no saby book...

1. Letter from Eyo Honesty II to Commander Raymond, Man-of-War Ship 'Spy', Creek Town, 1842, cited in H.M. Waddell, *Twenty-Nine Years in West Indies and Central Africa: A Review of Missionary Work and Adventure, 1827–1858* (London: Frank Cass, 2nd edn, 1970), p. 664.
2. E.U. Aye, *Old Calabar through the Centuries* (Calabar: Hope Waddell Press, 1967), p. 116.
3. Of related interest here would be Harold Turner's article entitled 'The Hidden Power of the Whites: The Secret Religion Withheld from the Primal Peoples', in *Religious Innovation in Africa* (Boston: G.K. Hall, 1979), pp. 271-88, where he describes how several 'primal' peoples viewed the Bible as the source of European power, particularly those parts held back from them.

It no fit they pass boy';[1] 'Book [Bible] no good for women, and women no fit saby book'.[2] The missionaries sought to show that educated women made the best wives and mothers and that girls should seek salvation as well as boys and 'know the word of God for themselves'.[3] Yet it was only in 1850 that women (particularly those of higher social ranking) first attended church in Calabar. Subsequent attendance was sporadic until 1868 when the men went away to war. During their absence women started attending church regularly, a trend which was not to be reversed.

Despite the missionaries' concern for the welfare and education of the women, it should be noted that they aimed to produce women to fulfil the complementary roles of wives and mothers rather than the more primary and literate roles of public officials and government workers. Women were often ministered to in their compounds by the missionary wives.[4] This more informal approach emphasized the importance of high standards of morality and hygiene and the acquisition of appropriate skills for Christian women, together with basic Christian teachings. It is noteworthy that this pattern has persisted in women's ways of worship in many parts of southern Nigeria in the form of compound healing activities, house fellowships and women's organizations such as the Mother's Union. In these contexts women have been able to circumvent male- and text-dominated forms of worship and deal with their own religious needs.

Variations in the roles ascribed to women naturally occurred on account of the differing missionary traditions and their cultural heritages. But even those missions which employed female mission agents, such as the Presbyterian and Roman Catholic churches, were still nurturing women to be passive reproducers of mission tradition (epitomized in the Sunday school teacher) and to be more subtle influences on their men and offspring (as the model Christian wife). One wonders how different the situation might have been if the great Scottish missionary, Ma Mary Slessor, who worked in the Cross River

1. Waddell, *Twenty-Nine Years in West Indies and Central Africa*, p. 346.
2. Aye, *Old Calabar through the Centuries*, p. 119.
3. Waddell, *Twenty-Nine Years in West Indies and Central Africa*, p. 346.
4. See R.I.J. Hackett, 'Beyond Afternoon Tea: Images and Roles of Missionary Women in South-Eastern Nigeria', in P. Kulp (ed.), *Women Missionaries and Cultural Change* (Issues in Third World Studies, 40; Williamsburg, VA: Department of Anthropology, William and Mary College, 1987).

area from 1876–1916, had divulged the secret notes she wrote in the margins of her Bible. At the place where St Paul advocates the subjection of women to their husbands she wrote, 'Na! Na! Paul, laddie! This will not do!'[1] Her own life reflected an ongoing and heart-searching negotiation of Victorian mores, local traditions and her own driving concern for women's rights and welfare.

For some Nigerian women the avenues open to them in the Christian church were too limited and they nurtured even greater dreams of religious self-determination. A number of women from the 1920s onwards branched out on their own or were instrumental in forming new churches, usually as the result of a crisis in their lives and an attendant visionary experience. Among such women were Christianah Abiodun Akinsowon (of the Cherubim and Seraphim movement), Agnes Okoli or Mama Odozi-Obodo (Christ Holy Church), Theresa T.A. Offiong (Holy Chapel of Miracles), Maddie Raymond (Mount Olive Church of Christ), Theresa S.U. Inyang (Church of God Lamentation of Jehovah) and more recently Lady Evangelist Margaret Bolanle Odeleke (Christ Message Ministry) and Lady Evangelist Dorcas Olaniyi (Agbala Daniel), to name those I am most familiar with.

From my experience of these indigenous spiritual churches (or 'white garment churches' as many of them are known) they tend to lay emphasis on healing, prophecy and pastoral care rather than biblical literacy and church growth. Yet they readily resort to the Bible as a source of legitimation for their activities. In cases where the women founders and leaders have received little or no Western education, they still incorporate the Bible in their liturgy. The late founder or Blessed Spiritual Mother of the Holy Chapel of Miracles in Calabar preferred the use of a Jehovah's Witnesses' Bible because of the colour illustrations and the simplified text. Early in 1991 I encountered a prophetess, not in Nigeria but in western Ghana, who had just established her own healing compound and branch of the Church of the Twelve Apostles, a well-known spiritual church in the area. She admitted to being a farmer with no school education, but was proud to

1.   J. Buchan, *The Expendable Mary Slessor* (Edinburgh: St Andrew's Press, 1980), cited in R.I.J. Hackett, 'Sacred Parodoxes: Women and Religious Plurality in Nigeria', in Y. Haddad and E. Findly (eds.), *Women, Religion and Social Change* (Albany, NY: State University of New York Press, 1985), pp. 247-71.

show me the Bible centrally located in their ritual space—distinguished by its symbolic power rather than its theological content. A related example which comes to mind is the practice in these churches of people sleeping on the Bible for protection or inspiration for their problems.[1] Pentecostalists and evangelicals may also use the Bible for apotropaic purposes, carrying it on their person and using it as a 'weapon' against satanic forces. The Bible may also be used as an object of divination, as reported to me by a woman whose friend consulted a local prophet over her desire to marry a certain man.[2] The prophet asked her to hold one end of the Bible, and he took the other until it shook. He then declared that the man would marry her if she performed the necessary sacrifices and vows.

Despite the greater authority and participation enjoyed by women in these spiritual churches (although some argue that this is no more than ceremonial authority[3]), ambivalent attitudes abound with regard to their perceived creative and destructive spiritual powers. Women are seen both as primary vehicles of the spirit and, because of their perceived uncleanness, as a source of spiritual pollution. In some churches, such as the Celestial Church of Christ, women are not supposed to handle the Bible during their menses and after childbirth. Likewise they are not allowed to read the Bible lessons in church nor preach (although they may now do so at outdoor revivals).

We also find replicated here the pattern of the older churches where women are given jurisdiction over other women and children (generally involving Bible instruction, story-telling and religious education), but are generally excluded from any serious Bible exegesis, theological exposition or cultural interpretation. Women's authority in the spiritual churches derives largely from their spiritual powers, but

---

1. An interesting contrast here, this time from the Cote d'Ivoire, is Marie Lalou's prohibition for her followers in the Deima Cult on reading and handling the Bible, which she held to be magical (cited by S.S. Walker, 'The Message as the Medium: The Harrist Churches of the Ivory Coast and Ghana', in B. Jules-Rosette [ed.], *The New Religions of Africa* [Norwood, NJ: Ablex Publishing Corporation, 1979], p. 48).

2. Interview with Charity Okorafor, April 11 1991.

3. This interpretation is particularly associated with B. Jules-Rosette. See, for example, 'Cultural Ambivalence and Ceremonial Leadership: The Role of Women in Africa's New Religions', in J.C.B. Webster and E.L. Webster (eds.), *The Church and Women in the Third World* (Philadelphia: Westminster Press, 1985), pp. 88-104.

there are signs of change as more educated and professional women join their ranks and exert an influence (directly or indirectly) on church doctrine. The Sole Spiritual Head of the Brotherhood of the Cross and Star, a large spiritual church with its headquarters in Calabar, is now firmly advocating the primary role of his deaconesses in preaching the Gospel. He emphasizes their ability to 'appreciate the gospel more than men' and to embody the godlike virtues of strength, obedience, love and fearlessness.[1] The red turban worn by the deaconesses assigns to them the power to preach the Word of God. Obu implies that men as 'tricksters and fornicators' have failed to practise the Gospel. He exhorts women to remember that 'in spirit you are all men'—a comment which reflects social conceptions of male strength. Incidentally, Obu's observation with regard to men's social and religious failings in contemporary Nigeria would be endorsed by many.

Turning to the main focus of this paper, let us now examine women's attitudes to and use of the Bible in the fast growing Pentecostal and evangelical movements. Pentecostal churches have been present in Nigeria since the 1930s in the form of the (British) Apostolic Church and the (American) Apostolic Faith, Assemblies of God, Faith Tabernacle and Foursquare Gospel Church, although there is evidence of a Pentecostal-type revival which predated the arrival of overseas Pentecostalist mission bodies. Evangelical para-church organizations such as the Scripture Union, the Student Christian Movement and the Christian Union became active in Nigerian schools and universities from the 1940s onwards.[2] But the real charismatic revival began in 1970 with the spread of teachings on and the experience of the baptism of the Holy Spirit, speaking in tongues and renewed evangelistic activities. Initially, women were not involved in the leadership of the charismatic renewal. However, since the locus of the revival (particularly the Protestant revival) was chiefly the campuses of Nigeria's higher educational institutions where female students were to be found in growing numbers, it was not particularly surprising to find women starting to play key roles by the 1980s. This, combined with the women pastors and evangelists being trained by the Pentecostal churches themselves, such as the Foursquare Gospel

1. O.O. Obu, 'You Are Apostles of God!', *The New Kingdom Deaconess* (Kalabar: The Brotherhood of the Cross and Star, n.d.), pp. 24-25.
2. See M.A. Ojo, 'The 1970 Charismatic Revival in Nigeria', *Thelia*, 3.2 (1990), pp. 4-9.

Church (founded by an American woman, Aimée Semple McPherson) and the Church of God Mission International at their All Nations for Christ Bible Institute in Benin City, as well as the increasingly popular husband and wife evangelical team, along American lines, have meant greater prominence for women. This provides us with more material with which to analyze and compare women's agency in a movement which is very Bible-centred and at times fundamentalist in orientation.

My first example is a woman, Dr (Mrs) Ebele Eko, a lecturer in the Department of English at the University of Calabar, who began making a name for herself as a producer and distributor of biblical tracts in the early 1980s. These tracts bore the stamp of her association with the Assemblies of God church and her American educational experience, being centred on biblical verses dealing with salvation, conversion and the Christian life. Ebele Eko, an articulate and charismatic woman, has been actively involved in student evangelism; at one time there was even a question of her establishing a separate body, the Evangelistic Church of the Redeemed, on campus. She is currently writing features on Christian life and marriage in the *Sunday Chronicle*.

A team of women academics at Obafemi Awolowo University in Ile-Ife has been producing a magazine entitled *The Virtuous Woman* since 1988. These women belong to a ministry known as 'Nigerian Women for Christ', which is concerned to portray a 'model of a Christian woman whom God wants to use to build the home and of course the nation—Nigeria which God loves so much'.[1] The publication which is 'intended to exhort, to edify, to educate and to point lost souls to Christ's saving grace' has as its motto a verse from the book of Proverbs, 'Every wise woman buildeth her house' (Prov. 14.1). In addition to articles on home life, health care, appearance and marriage, there are also expositions of biblical texts and Christian festivals.[2] One is struck by how biblically grounded the discussions are in

1. *The Virtuous Woman* 1.1 (1988). Cf. a similar movement launched in May 1991, known as Evangel Women International (the women's wing of the Grace Evangel Mission in Lagos) which aims to reach out to socially alienated women, such as single parents, divorcees, spinsters, through vocational skills, rehabilitation and leisure programmes, so as 'to minister to the total woman who would be relevant in the church, home and the society at large' (*The Guardian* [Lagos], May 29 1991).

2. For example I. Afolabi, 'For You at Easter', *The Virtuous Woman* 3.1 (March–May 1990), pp. 12-15.

their attempts to relate the Christian experience to the lives of contemporary Nigerian women.

The *Nigerian Christian Journal*, an interdenominational religious magazine whose motto is 'Preach the Word', is not aimed at an exclusively female readership, yet it is the product of a woman publisher and a woman editor. The publisher's lead article in issue 1.5 (1988) is entitled 'Acknowledgment of God's Calling' and is centred on the Bible verse, 'Where there is no vision, the people perish. . . ' (Prov. 29.18). Mrs Carole Sholesi recounts how a lawyer friend of hers was reading his Bible secretly until struck by the power of God to declare his conversion and embark on an active Christian life. Even in newspapers edited by men, such as *Life-Link: A Scripture Pasture Christian Weekly*, one finds general articles by women such as 'Growing in Grace' by Sister Toyin Fadimi.[1]

Another woman convinced not only of the spiritual potency of the Bible but also of its creative appeal is Theresa Luck Akinwale. An artist and art teacher by profession, she has opened a storefront 'gospel shop' in Ibadan known as the 'The Word of God Focus'. There she sells Bible verses which she has artistically reproduced in attractive frames. A young man is also on hand to deal with prayer requests and to read and discuss portions of the Bible.

Bible study features prominently in the activities of the newly founded Jesus Women Prayer Band Ministry in Benin City. Eunice Osagedie, a trained educationalist and a former Roman Catholic, began her 'deliverance ministry built strictly on the word of God', as she calls it, in 1987.[2] She describes the ministry as 'into the business of healing homes, healing marriages and really streamlining the word of God with regards to marriage'. As far as Eunice and I know, there is no other such ministry devoted entirely to women in Nigeria. There are now over 5000 members, mainly married women. They have branches in London, Birmingham and the US. They meet on Wednesday and Thursday evenings for Bible study, worship, counselling and evangelism. No men attend except for the annual marriage seminar. It is interesting to note that the concept of the ministry and its motto, 'We Have Seen Jesus', derive from the personal revelation

1.   *Life-Link: A Scripture Pasture Christian Weekly*, 4.13 (March 1991).

2.   See her account of the origins of the movement in their newly launched magazine *Beauty for Ashes* 1.1 (1991), p. 23.

of the founder, or coordinator as she is humbly known. This revelation led to a greater clarification of a biblical event, the discovery of the risen Christ by Mary Magdalene in Mark 16. Osagedie's interpretation of the encounter lends support to her conviction that women have a primary role to play in evangelism and deliverance and that they should be responsible for their own salvation and spiritual development.[1] She frequently cites as models the cases of those biblical women, for example Esther, the Samaritan woman and Mary Magdalene, who played key roles and to whom 'the greatest truths in Christianity' were revealed.

Let us now consider the significant role being played by the Bible as a template for women's identity and roles both within and beyond the church. With the centrality of the Word in the evangelical and Pentecostal movements, it is not surprising that a type of blueprint has emerged, with only slight variations (which I shall consider below). In preaching the Gospel to the world, women and men must join forces, especially given the urgency of the endtimes. Women may be vehicles of the spirit and receive spiritual gifts in the same way as men. Generally speaking those churches that emphasize the 'Full Gospel' do not enforce any (Levitican) taboos on women, as do many of the spiritual churches, with regard to menstruation and childbirth. They regard these as having been obviated by the prescriptions of the New Testament.

Variations occur over women's roles as preachers and pastors, whether they should be silent and uninvolved in church affairs (1 Cor. 14.34-35) or enjoy full equality and responsibility. A recurrent pattern is for women to play active roles in evangelizing, leading Bible study classes, preaching at outdoor crusades and revivals, directing music, fund-raising and assisting with church services and organization, but to be barred from exercising full responsibilities as pastors or heads of churches, not just because of biblical support, but for cultural reasons—arguments on the lines of 'our people are not yet ready for such changes'. Sometimes more practical reasons for these limitations have been adduced, as by W.F. Kumuyi, founder and General Superintendent of one of Nigeria's largest Pentecostal/holiness churches in Lagos, the Deeper Life Bible Church:

---

1. *Beauty for Ashes* 1.1 (1991), p. 24.

> I do not see that the Scripture goes against women ministering. I would
> see from the Scriptures that there is more for the men, because the women
> have a lot of things to do at home. We still want them to take care of the
> family and children. We wouldn't want their ministry in the church to
> conflict with the training of their children at home.[1]

In several cases women derive authority to speak and act by virtue of
co-dependency, that is to say through their husband's status and
authority. There are a number of 'wives' on the national circuit who
speak frequently at revivals, seminars and the like, particularly those
that address women's or marital issues. I attended a recent conference
in Ile-Ife organized by the Full Gospel Business Men's Fellowship
International on 'The Christian Woman in these Endtimes'. Mrs
Tokunbo Olubi Johnson and Mrs Folu Adeboye, wives of, respectively, a well-known Pentecostal church founder (Scripture Pasture in
Ibadan) and church leader (Redeemed Christian Church of God in
Lagos) were keynote speakers. In some cases the wife may become a
popular speaker and authority in her own right, as in the case of
Blessing Boye, the co-founder with her husband of Firebrands
Evangelistic Ministries in Ile-Ife and a powerful young preacher who
received pastoral training in the Foursquare Gospel Bible College in
Lagos.

Some churches impose limitations on women studying and interpreting the Bible, restricting them to women's or children's groups
alone. The Deeper Life Bible Church, mentioned above, initially
ordained women and allowed them to head churches. Now they are
limited to serving as Women's Representatives in the various zones.
Biodun Kumuyi (the founder's wife) serves as the Women's
Coordinator and leads the women's representatives in 'Bible study on
such characters as Miriam and Ruth, but also practical matters such as
setting tables, making the home comfortable, intimacy with God even
though they are busy, and accidents in the home'.[2]

The Christ Apostolic Church is also firmly against women
preaching and serving as pastors. But, interestingly, a number of
strong, independent women evangelists have emerged from its ranks,
challenging the expulsion of women from the pulpit. The most well-
known of these women is Dorcas Olaniyi, the founder of Agbala

1.   Cited in A. Isaacson, *Deeper Life* (London: Hodder & Stoughton, 1990),
p. 102.

2.   Cited in Isaacson, *Deeper Life*, p. 102.

Daniel and well known to television viewers in western Nigeria. The 'lady evangelist', as she is known, openly addresses such issues as divorce (her second [clergyman] husband divorced her because of the conflict between their spiritual careers) and women's religious responsibilities. She strongly advocates that women realize their full religious and leadership potential and renounce ungodly husbands (although she does still endorse the man as leader of the household). In contrast to Olaniyi, Lady Evangelist Odeleke, founder of Agbala Olurun Ki i bati or Christ Message Ministry, still regards herself as part of the fold of the Christ Apostolic Church and as not having the status of a pastor, but in reality she heads a successful ministry and is a forceful proponent of women's speaking out spiritually. In her response to a question from a journalist regarding the Pauline injunction for women to be silent in church, she tendered a contextual response, somewhat uncommon in such movements:

> People don't understand that Bible verse. Gospelling is more of a woman's job than a man's. Right from creation, woman was made from the bone nearest to the heart. This was why Eve could convince Adam to eat the fruit. Even in the New Testament we saw the Marys. So women are basically kind-hearted, and conscientious in anything they do. Men think about themselves too much, this explains why most of the activities of the lady evangelists and prophetesses were not recorded in the Bible. Still there was Phoebe, Priscilla, and the rest of them who founded churches, prophesied and taught. You cannot profess to have the spirit of God in you and keep silent. The fire of spirit will be so hot in you that you will speak out. This was Paul's solution to the particular problem in the church at that time.[1]

In discussing her role as a woman preacher, she unabashedly points to the problems in male-led churches, namely corruption and adultery. Nor is she alone in advocating female religious leadership, given the organizational and financial skills that women acquire in the home. Eunice Osagedie, of the Jesus Women Prayer Band Ministry, is keen to emphasize the privileged position of women who, despite supposedly causing the fall of the human race, were the vehicle of salvation (through Mary) and of the revelation of the greatest truths in Christianity (Jn 4.23; 11.25; 29.17).[2] In the Celestial Church of

1. 'Designer Turned Evangelist', *The Nigerian Christian Journal* 1.5 (1988), p. 22.
2. See the highlights of her 3rd Annual Marriage Seminar (brochure).

Christ, a large and well-established spiritual church, an interesting challenge to the limitations imposed on women in terms of preaching and Bible study is currently emerging from the student's fellowship, known as FOCUS, which has a strong evangelical/Pentecostal orientation. Male and female students engage in active Bible study on campus during the week and then go to the branches of the church in the town on Sundays where they conduct short Bible study classes and give talks on evangelism. These are often led by women.[1]

Nigerian women's images of themselves are strongly conditioned by negative attitudes and stereotypes, being often blamed by their menfolk and the press for marital instability, prostitution and economic failures.[2] Single women (particularly those in the choir)[3] are singled out as potential Jezebels[4] and women in general are considered in many quarters as more susceptible to possession by evil spirits and as in need of deliverance.[5] There are obvious continuities here with traditional perceptions of women's powers and their propensity for and vulnerability to witchcraft.

It is perhaps in response to such attitudes and beliefs, together with more general fears about social dislocation and the breakdown of traditional morals and family life, that many Pentecostal women have been actively engaged, through a variety of media, in the articulation and construction of a 'virtuous woman' model. The ideal Christian woman is one who is the 'help meet' of the man and who accepts his

1.   Interview with Esther Abaton, a student of nursing at Obafemi Awolowo University, Ile-Ife, May 30 1991. It should be added, however, that the student organization has been proscribed by the official church body, although it still continues to operate and have an influence.

2.   See C. Obbo, *African Women: Their Struggle for Economic Independence* (London: Zed Press, 1980), pp. 4-9.

3.   There is popularly held to be a close link between water spirits and fine music.

4.   See especially an article by Kumuyi on 'Backsliding' in his newspaper *Deeper Life* 2.7 (February 1991), p. 8, where he writes of the need to 'flush out' all women 'with undue influence in the Church, who are prayerless, ungodly and backslidden, but by their voice wield a lot of influence on pastors and other ministers'. He cites at length Prov. 2.16-19, 'to deliver thee from the strange woman, even from the stranger which flattereth with her words. . . '

5.   See, for example, Evangelist V. Eko's *Exposition on Water Spirits* (Warri, 1983) which details the perils of the (predominantly female) mammy water (or mamy wata) spirits whose demonic allure is feared by all.

authority and leadership.[1] As the 'handmaid of the Lord' she must be submissive, ready, obedient, able and born-again.[2] This model draws heavily on biblical prescriptions for women. It is also supplemented by advice about appearance, cooking, hygiene and health care such as would appeal to the educated and aspiring Nigerian woman. There is a strong sense in which women who belong to these movements perceive them as more modern and progressive, free from the shackles of tradition, taboos and superstition. It is indeed arguable in another light that religious movements centred on the spirit offer greater mobility and avenues of expression than those generated by centuries of androcentric historical tradition. At very least, the Bible serves as an important interpretive mechanism for women, enabling them to make sense of fortunate and unfortunate experiences in their lives and eventually control and transform them ('the Lord led me to the book of...'). At times this translates into a simple dualism between the hand of God or the hand of Satan at work in their lives. 'I knew it was the work of Satan the devil, for the Bible makes me to understand in the book of Eph. 6.1-13 that "the battle we fight is not against flesh and blood but against principalities and powers, against the rulers of the darkness of this world"', wrote one woman whose children were burned as the result of an electrical accident.[3]

Yet the very conservatism of the model of the 'virtuous woman' may serve to perpetuate the repression, subordination and suffering of women. Prayer and Bible study are the means advocated to effect transformation rather than social activism. The grounding of the discourse in the domestic context effectively undermines the public roles of women. As long as Nigeria's Christian bookshops and video stores continue to be flooded by religious literature from the United States with its conservative theology, biblical literalism and opposition to women's liberation, the situation seems unlikely to change noticeably. An association of African Women Theologians is gaining strength, but their more radical critique is currently limited to academics, female clergy and religious professionals.

1. See, for example, 'Your Marriage Counsellor', *Herald of the Last Days* 35 (n.d.), pp. 9-11 (a publication circulated by an independent British Pentecostalist based in Ilesha, Reverend S.G. Elton).

2. F. Faleye, 'Behold! The Handmaid of the Lord', *The Virtuous Woman* 3.3 (December 1990–February 1991), p. 8.

3. *Beauty for Ashes*, pp. 5-6.

There appears to be some irony in a situation where women now enjoy greater access to the Bible, in fact no longer rely on male intermediaries (some of them rather turn to American women inter-preters/evangelists[1] or their own resources) but because of their theo-logical stance end up by largely perpetuating the status quo. Nonetheless, we should not decry the greater access of women to the Bible through the medium of the newer evangelical and Pentecostal movements, nor their far greater inclusion in Christian evangelism and missionary work than was hitherto known in Nigeria. Nor should we ignore the growing output by women of Christian inspirational and exegetical literature. For the most part this literature does not seek to challenge the status quo nor is it gender-specific, but it is both a source and manifestation of the revival of a new found self-confidence for women and awareness of their dignity. Such convic-tions may serve to propel women (somewhat unintentionally) into positions of higher authority and create new avenues for creative action and self-realization, both within the social and religious domains.

The focus of this paper has been on the greater use of the Bible by women in the rapidly growing evangelical and Pentecostal movements in southern Nigeria. I would emphasize in closing that this chapter of Nigeria's religious history, with the particular interest it has for us here in terms of the relationship between women and the Bible, cannot be seen in isolation. I have tried to point to the roots and configuration of forces, both social and cultural, contemporary and historical, of the ambivalent attitudes to women and of women which have determined their use of the Bible. I would single out in retrospect two main reasons for this trend of greater biblical use by women: first, the theological emphasis of these movements; the importance of soul-winning, the eschatology of the 'endtime', and the charismatic experience; and secondly the cultural and socio-economic reasons, chiefly, the increased literacy and professional achievements of Nigerian women. The Pentecostal revival is experiencing a strong

1.   Examples of such women are Reverend Coletta Harris Vaughn of the Go Tell It Ministries, Michigan (a key speaker at the Christian Women Fellowship International in Benin City in 1990), and Reverend Jean Thompson of the Harvest Church International, Washington, DC.

momentum in many parts of Africa, eclipsing evangelicalism, condemning the spiritual churches and challenging mainline Christianity. My paper is but an initial exploration of one aspect of this highly significant yet very under-researched phenomenon.

Haunting the Margins of History: Toni Morrison's *Beloved*

Linda Anderson

The sacred occupies a space beyond or outside history. In a secular world the sacred points to limits, borders, an unnamed outside; it suggests the tenuous nature of our conceptions of history, language and meaning. It could be said that women, who have been repressed by history, have a special interest in exploring these limits, and I therefore want to examine the idea of the sacred through recent writing by women, in particular Toni Morrison's novel *Beloved*. However, I want to use Marguerite Duras as a starting point and in particular her wartime diary *La Douleur*, first published in 1985 and seemingly rescued at that time from her own loss of memory. She 'found' this diary, she tells us, in a couple of exercise books and while she could recognize her handwriting and the details of the story she had no recollection of ever having written it. The diary records the period of waiting she endured after the war had ended for her husband to return from a concentration camp—a time, if you like, which extends beyond a conclusion. She links this first narrative to two other stories included in the same volume which she introduces with this comment:

> Thérèse is me. The person who tortures the informer is me. So also is the one who feels like making love to Ter, the member of the Militia. Me. I give you the torturer along with the rest of the texts. Learn to read them properly: they are sacred.[1]

Julia Kristeva has described all Duras's writing as writing 'without catharsis'. She goes on to comment: that, 'with neither cure nor God, without value or beauty other than the malady itself, seized at the site of its essential fissure, Duras's art is perhaps as minimally cathartic as

---

1. M. Duras, *La Douleur* (trans. B. Bray; London: Flamingo, 1987), p. 115.

art can be'.[1] Kristeva points to the way that Duras deprives us of any promise of a beyond, any relief from suffering. In the ambivalent time of her writing—a writing which seems to enclose its own future within itself—we never arrive at a point where we can achieve sufficient distance to look from 'afar' through the emotions of 'pity and fear' at what has occurred. The lack of purification—to return to the original meaning of the term 'catharsis'—in Duras's writing must also be related to the way she offers us meanings contaminated by a lack of boundaries, the difficulty of achieving separation. She suggests how fragile the distinctions are between innocence and guilt, love and loss, desire and indifference, and she makes both herself and the reader complicit in the 'malady'—to use Kristeva's term—she describes: 'I give you the torturer along with the rest of the texts'. To read these texts properly is to read them with a simultaneity which is also, of course, impossible; to read them with an awareness of how narrative produces and thereby also limits meaning. What makes these texts sacred, I suggest, is the way they present, are present at, the dangerous brink of our psychic lives, the point at which meaning and its dissolution, signification and the breakdown of meaning or madness, intersect.

In order to pursue further these ideas about the sacred I want to turn now to Julia Kristeva whom I have already cited in connection with Duras. In her book *Powers of Horror* Kristeva talks about the sacred as constituted through its relationship with the abject which it attempts to exclude or to purify. The abject, according to Kristeva, precedes the emergence of 'objects' to which the subject relates from a position of autonomy or separateness. It is the pre-symbolic and thus unrepresentable fear situated at the point where the subject first splits from the body of the mother and finds within a precarious and terrifying gap the space in which to constitute its own identity. Thus the abject is also all that threatens the unity of the subject and the boundaries of the body: it is what is composite, in between, ambiguous. The abject, for Kristeva, always accompanies the sacred, coincides with it; for if the sacred is constituted through its attempt to ward off what threatens or defiles it—the abject or the fear of engulfment by the maternal body—it could also be said to be rooted in it. For Kristeva, the sacred is divided, a 'two-sided formation': 'one aspect is defensive

---

1. J. Kristeva, 'The Pain of Sorrow in the Modern World: The Works of Marguerite Duras', *PMLA* 102 (1987), p. 141.

and socializing, the other shows fear and indifferentiation'. The sacred, therefore, in part, involves a confrontation with the pre-symbolic or the feminine. In this aspect it is

> like a lining, more secret still and invisible, non-representable, oriented toward those uncertain spaces of unstable identity, toward the fragility— both threatening and fusional—of the archaic dyad, toward the non-separation of subject/object, on which language has no hold but one woven of fright and repulsion.[1]

The sacred is drawn to the very boundaries of meaning and places both the subject and language at risk.

Toni Morrison's novel *Beloved*[2] is a novel about slavery. Set in the period after the civil war when slavery, at least in a legal sense, had been abolished, it looks back, through the characters' memories and the stories they tell to each other, to the era before. The novel carefully refers to and uses the available historical information about this period; indeed Morrison has specifically acknowledged that she based the novel on a real incident that she read about: 'A story I came across about a woman called Margaret Garner who had escaped from Kentucky, I think, into Cincinnati with four children... And she was a kind of *cause célèbre* among abolitionists in 1855 or 56 because she tried to kill the children when she was caught. She killed one of them just as in the novel'.[3] But *Beloved* is not just about recorded history; it is also about history's absences, about how what has been repressed historically and unremembered can return to haunt us, troubling the boundaries of what is known. 'That unrecorded past,' Frieda Forman writes, 'is always with us and its absence strikes at odd, unsuspecting moments.'[4] The unrecorded past Forman is referring to is the missing history of women,[5] but for Morrison there are other absences too: the

---

1.   J. Kristeva, *Powers of Horror* (trans. L.S. Roudiez; Columbia: Columbia University Press, 1982), p. 58.

2.   T. Morrison, *Beloved* (London: Chatto & Windus, 1987). All references to this novel are included in the text.

3.   Cited by M. Rothstein, 'Morrison Defends Women', *New York Times*, 26 August 1987.

4.   In F. Johles Forman with C. Sowton (eds.), *Taking Our Time* (London: Pergamon Press 1989), p. 8.

5.   See my essay 'The Re-imagining of History in Contemporary Women's Fiction', where I also discuss *Beloved* (in L. Anderson [ed.], *Plotting Change* [Stratford Upon Avon Series; London: Edward Arnold, 1990]).

only partially acknowledged sufferings of slavery which despite the existence of some slave narratives have never really been adequately explored on an imaginative level; the prehistory of Afro-Americans in Africa and the devastations of the Middle Passage which forms both a physical and a temporal link between the previous two experiences. In attempting to find a way of expressing this material and in probing the bonds of mother and daughter through the taboo topic of infanticide, Morrison is also trying to speak the unspeakable, to approach a horror which threatens the very existence of the subject. 'The trauma of racism,' Morrison has written, 'is for the racist and the victim, the severe fragmentation of the self, and has always seemed to me a cause (not a symptom) of psychosis.'[1]

Beloved is a difficult and challenging text which, while historically based, resists the linear structure of historical narrative. The past is, rather, coterminous with the present in the novel, continually invading it, or hovering at its edges, hinting at meanings which have been forgotten or repressed. For Sethe, the mother and main protagonist of the novel, time, as she tells her daughter Denver, cannot always be distinguished from the physical reality and permanence of place:

> Where I was before I came here, that place is real. It's never going away. Even if the whole farm—every tree and grass blade of it dies. The picture is still there and what's more, if you go there—you who was never there—if you go there and stand in the place where it was, it will happen again; it will be there for you, waiting for you. So, Denver, you can't never go there. Never. Because even though it's all over—over and done with—it's going to always be there waiting for you. That's how come I had to get my children out. No matter what (p. 36).

Sweet Home Farm and Sethe's experience of slavery are presented as ominously indestructible; even though they are 'over', part of time which advances linearly, they are still 'there', existing in another dimension, a timeless place where their power never diminishes. For Sethe their horrifying 'reality' is greater than her own capacity to remember; they will go on existing, therefore, whether she remembers them or not.

Beloved's return, the return of the child Sethe killed in order to save her from slavery, functions in the novel as the return of what

---

1.   T. Morrison, 'Unspeakable Things Unspoken: The Afro-American Presence in American Literature', *Michigan Quarterly Review* 28.1 (1989), pp. 1-34.

cannot be remembered, a repressed memory which in 'real', albeit ghostly, form is haunting Sethe and others at the beginning of the novel. The daughter who has been absent, killed by an excess of maternal love—a love which has become distorted—and by the dehumanizing conditions of slavery, breaks into the symbolic as both disturbance and desire. For Morrison, Beloved's entry into the novel seems to have been born out of the need to provide another viewpoint on Sethe's conviction that she had to 'get [her] children out. No matter what'. Killing her child in these circumstances is, according to Morrison, understandable, but it also suggests pathology, a love with no boundaries which assumes rights over others and displaces the self.[1] Questions of blame or justification in relation to what Sethe does, however, lie outside the possibility of what can be told (what is the meaning of motherhood under slavery?) and can only, perhaps, be enacted in the narrative through the relational disruption represented by Beloved and the past, which both must and cannot be answered:

> She [Denver] had begun to notice that even when Beloved was quiet, dreamy, minding her own business, Sethe got her going again. Whispering, muttering some justification, some bit of clarifying information to Beloved to explain what it had been like, and why, and how come. It was as though Sethe didn't really want forgiveness given; she wanted it refused (p. 252).

Beloved, however, not only highlights the complexity of Sethe's action, she also brings a 'bottomless longing' into the text, an insatiable thirst. She seems to embody the daughter's desire for the mother, a desire which has been unlived and unsatisfied; she also stimulates the desires of the other characters in the novel and their own sense of longing and of lack. In the lyrical monologues which form the centre of the novel Denver, Sethe and Beloved all voice the same desire to possess the Beloved: 'She is mine'. But that desire springs first of all from the deprivation they share as daughters, the loss of a relationship to the mother. In these passages Morrison seems to be exploring the relationship between mother and daughter within a specific set of historical meanings, under the special conditions of slavery, but she is also exploring it as an analogy for historical meaning, the repressed and forgotten meanings which have been excluded from the symbolic, from history as authoritative narrative

---

1. Cited by Rothstein, 'Morrison Defends Women'.

about the past. In Beloved's monologue which fuses the language of the daughter, returned from the dead, with the language of a survivor from a (factual) slave ship, both identity and body become fragmented; Beloved inhabits a psychic space—in Kristeva's terms the place of abjection—where the boundaries between inside and outside, self and other, are insecure; where the subject, painfully struggling to identify itself, could dissolve again into the surrounding sea:

> We are not crouching now   we are standing but my legs are like my dead man's eyes   I cannot fall because there is no room to   the men without skin are making loud noises   I am not dead   the bread is sea-colored   I am too hungry to eat it   the sun closes my eyes   those able to die are in a pile   I cannot find my man   the one whose teeth I have loved   a hot thing the little hill of dead people   a hot thing   the men without skin push them through with poles   the woman is there with the face I want   the face that is mine   they fall into the sea which is the colour of bread (p. 211).

This traumatized language is also the trauma of language encountering the impossibility of representation: where there is no settled distinction between self and other the subject struggles ambivalently and unsuccessfully to make images cohere within language. It is as if this history, the unspoken and unspeakable history of slavery, can only be recorded by Morrison situating her writing in that horrifying gap of the abject, at the very boundary where language identity and narrative structure begin to break down.

In offering *Beloved* as a sacred text I am making a case for the sacred, therefore, as neither mystification or idealization: although Morrison explores the irrational, Beloved's ghostly haunting and return from the dead, this is the way Morrison is able to connect her writing to history. Instead of attempting to find transcendence through writing, the conditions through which history can finally erase itself, Morrison seeks instead those very moments, the places of risk and terror, where the body fails to constitute itself in words.

Morrison's final comment in the novel that 'it was not a story to pass on' (p. 275) is of course ambiguous, for while acknowledging the reasons why Beloved may be best forgotten, the narrator *is* passing the story on, giving words to Beloved's fading, ghostly traces. Like Duras who relinquishes authority and control over her diary by surrounding it with her own forgetfulness, Morrison also seems to refuse to fix her text's meanings in her own deliberate act of authorship. Her novel is not, Morrison implies, sacrosanct, and if it is sacred it is only so if the meaning of that term is also understood to be fragile and unstable.

Part 5: Theology

Introduction to Part 5: Theology

Jon Davies and Isabel Wollaston

Sociology is an essentially modern discipline; it developed as an attempt to understand the transformations of the world in which the peasantry became proletariat, in which huge cities appeared, in which great engines of iron and steam vastly enhanced human capacity to regulate and exploit Nature. The subject matter of sociology was therefore the study of the modern era, that is to say of a world equipped with an immediate and extensive and quantitative archive. Social change could be and was both experienced and measured as it happened; it was a contemporary matter.

This immediate experience and quantification of social change clearly does not apply to earlier and long-gone epochs or societies, and in many ways the task of 'seeing' those societies is a task of inferring social changes from surviving religious texts which were themselves, arguably, artefacts of those very changes. There is clearly a risk of tautological self-indulgence in a sociological exegesis of such texts: this text changed and the nature of this change is imputed from the text. This risk can only be avoided by a powerful and empathetic form of scholarship; powerful in the range of deployed sources, and empathetic via an immersion in the continuing vitalities of the historical moment and tradition. Both the contributors in this last section—Jacob Neusner and Michael Mach—exhibit this power and empathy as they present an account of complex textual changes in the Jewish 'canon' which can plausibly be related to parallel reorderings of life within the Jewish 'nation' and in its relationship with its neighbours. Michael Mach, for example, argues that 'the roots of the apocalyptic movement are connected with profound changes in the Jewish society of the Second Temple period':—opposition to the Jerusalem Temple cult; opposition to a rich and monarchical and high-priestly ruling class; and opposition to Hellenistic and foreign domination over the

Jewish people. Mach shows also how the prophetic patterns of legitimation adopted by the apocalyptic leaders had the effect of turning
them into an elite within an elite; Mach quotes Grünwald to the effect
that 'the apocalyptics define themselves as the elected ones within the
elected People', separated away from the rest of Israel in the desert
community of Qumran. In this way, says Mach, arguments about
prophetic or other forms of legitimations of canon can be seen as
arguments both about inter-group boundaries and intra-group
hierarchy.

Jacob Neusner sweeps us all along in a magisterial treatise on the
differences between the Jewish and the Christian construction of a
religious canon—although Neusner very carefully points out that the
Bavli is not a canon in the same sense as is the Christian Bible because
'revelation in the Bavli does not reach closure. The Judaic Torah
never closed'. Behind his (mainly textual) paper, Neusner 'sees' a
history of the two developing religions, one (the Christian) increasingly in a position not only to promulgate but also to enforce a fixed
and authoritative canon, the other (the Jewish) less securely based in
the secular world, but able by some extraordinary act of hubris
(Neusner's term) to effect radical and thorough-going theological
changes, while presenting them as nothing more than restatements of
tradition. The intertwining trajectories of these two religions make
up, of course, and for better or for worse, much of the more tragic
side of the story of the sociology of sacred texts!

The Social Implications of Scripture-Interpretation in Second Temple Judaism

Michael Mach

I

The Jewish Bible, that is the Christian Old Testament, has not always been 'sacred Scripture' in the sense in which the present generation uses this term. The traditions of old allowed for a free use, even rewriting, of scriptural texts, in a period when Christianity was not yet in existence, or had only begun to take its first steps in history.[1] In the crucial period which we call the Second Jewish Commonwealth (roughly speaking the late Persian, Hellenistic and early Roman periods) at least some of those books which are today held to be 'canonical' were freely used, interpreted and retold.[2] Others seem to date from this period. Contemporary biblical hermeneutics incorporates, among other approaches, one which depends upon what might be called a 'second revelation'. By 'second revelation' I mean the phenomenon whereby a fresh interpretation of an older scripture is offered, with the implication that this interpretation reveals the 'true' sense of the passage. The 'second' interpretation is held to constitute a further enlightenment from God. Such a process could be described as actualizing the 'true' meaning of the original text through divinely

---

1. See especially M. Fishbane, *Biblical Interpretation in Ancient Israel* (Oxford: Clarendon Press, repr., 1989 [1985]); for a more general, but nevertheless stimulating, survey, see J.L. Kugel, 'Early Interpretation: The Common Background of Later Forms of Biblical Exegesis', in J.L. Kugel and R.A. Greer, *Early Biblical Interpretation* (Library of Early Christianity, 3: Philadelphia), pp. 11-106.

2. See my 'Geleitwort' to Y. Amir's *Studien zum antiken Judentum* (Beitrage zur Enforschung des Alten Testaments und des Antiken Judentums, 2; Frankfurt am Main, 1985), pp. i-vi.

inspired exegesis. One example of what is meant by a 'second revelation' would be Daniel's interpretation of Jer. 25.11-2 in Dan. 9.2, a passage that is discussed in more detail below. Alternatively, perhaps, this new approach to Scripture is itself a response to sociological change.[1]

To be clear from the outset: interpretation of *our* sacred Scripture is not a process which begins only after a 'canon', in the full sense of the word, has emerged. There were already interrelations between biblical traditions in biblical times, and these found their way into the biblical texts. One outstanding example of a rewritten biblical text is incorporated in the canon: 1 and 2 Chronicles.[2]

At this point, it is important to note that the interpreters have often, though not exclusively, been prophets, such as Hosea or Ezekiel. Prophets might be considered 'inspired' persons. Indeed, in the biblical prophecies there are still some hints of the prophet's claim to have access to the heavenly realm and therefore to divine wisdom. This is clearly the case with Michaiah ben Imlah (1 Kgs 22.19) who, as part of his prophetic answer, reports that he saw the Holy One sitting upon his throne and that he, so to speak, attended the meeting of the heavenly council. This tradition can be seen in several places, for example Jer. 23.18. The wise men make a similar claim when they respond to

1. It should be noted that the theological impact of the same theory is immense. This part of the problem will be dealt with in a future article of mine. Here an attempt is made to treat the theological issues only as necessary background information. The notes are accordingly intended to give only the first keys. Other important aspects of the new theory of Scripture interpretation are dealt with in a series of publications by I. Grünwald; see his *Apocalyptic and Merkavah Mysticism* (Arbeiten zur Geschichte des Antiken Judentums und Urchristentums; Leiden: Brill, 1980), pp. 20ff. See also his 'Two Types of Jewish Esoteric Literature in the Time of the Mishna and Talmud', in *From Apocalypticism to Gnosticism: Studies in Apocalypticism, Merkavah Mysticism and Gnosticism* (Beiträge zur Erforschung des Alten Testaments und des Antiken Judentums, 14; Frankfurt am Main, 1988), as well as his '"Knowledge and Vision": Towards a Clarification of Two Gnostic Concepts in Light of their Alleged Origins', in *From Apocalypticism to Gnosticism*, pp. 65-123, esp. pp. 76, 80; needless to say, my own views regarding the Pseudepigrapha are based upon his and I owe to him not a few comments in this paper.

2. See further G.W.E. Nickelsburg, 'The Bible Rewritten and Expanded', in M.E. Stone (ed.), *Compendia Rerum Iudaicarum ad Novum Testamentum*. Section 2, Vol. II *Jewish Writings of the Second Temple Period: Apocrypha, Pseudepigrapha, Qumran Sectarian Writings, Philo, Josephus* (Philadelphia: Fortress Press, 1984), pp. 89-156.

the king's demand for an interpretation of his dream with the words: 'The thing that the king is asking is too difficult, and no one can reveal it to the king except the gods, whose dwelling is not with mortals' (Dan. 2.11).[1] Yet the Jewish wise man Daniel provides the 'revelation' requested by the king.

Prophetic inspiration is that of an outstanding person addressing the community or its leaders. Even when a prophet makes use of older traditions, he does so as a poet. He uses certain pictures which he assumes will be understood by his audience. Normally, these traditions are not 'Scripture' and are not taken from it.[2]

With Daniel, however, we witness a development: he is prophetically interpreting a prior scriptural tradition. In Dan. 9.2 the prophet specifically refers to a prior and, we must assume, acknowledged portion of Scripture: 'I Daniel perceived in the books the number of years that, according to the word of the LORD to the prophet Jeremiah, must be fulfilled'. The portion of Scripture to which Daniel alludes is Jer. 25.11-2. After his prayer, Daniel receives the required answer from the angel Gabriel who is sent to him for this purpose.[3] In other words, the angel Gabriel is not only employed to interpret a vision (which would be quite normal in later biblical writings), he also offers an exegesis of written Scripture. This is done in the second part of the book of Daniel, that is, in the very section which contains apocalyptic material.

As regards individual verses, exactly the same attitude is to be found elsewhere in apocalyptic writing; for example, in *2 Bar.* 4.3-4. God comforts the prophet over the destruction of Jerusalem: 'Or do you think that this is the city of which I said, "on the palms of my hands have I carved you?" [Isa. 49.16]. It is not this building that is in

---

1. See especially Fishbane, *Biblical Interpretation*, pp. 477ff.; for a different approach, see J. Blenkinsopp, 'Interpretation and the Tendency to Sectarianism: An Aspect of Second Temple History', in E.P. Sanders, A.I. Baumgarten and A. Mendelson (eds.), *Jewish and Christian Self-Definition. II. Aspects of Judaism in the Graeco–Roman Period* (London: SCM Press, 1981), pp. 1-26 (and notes on pp. 229-309).

2. As, for example, Hosea's recourse to Jacob's struggle (Genesis 32) in Hos. 12.4-5, or his interpretations of the wilderness traditions now contained in Exodus and Numbers. Yet these texts were not Scripture in Hosea's time and it is unlikely that he knew any texts like those which have since become 'canonical'.

3. See Blenkinsopp, 'Interpretation and Sectarianism', p. 10, for further remarks in connection with the *angelus interpres*.

your midst now; it is that which will be revealed'.[1] Two elements of this short passage merit attention. First, the same God who spoke to the prophet Isaiah now provides a definitive interpretation of the verse under consideration. Secondly, this divine clarification is more than mere interpretation: it corrects a previous and, it seems, already accepted understanding of the biblical phrase. Yet it is crucial for our discussion that the author of *2 Baruch* presents this new interpretation as coming from God himself. As a consequence, the 'second' interpretation is not only legitimated, it attains the status of divine revelation, as does the angelic revelation in Daniel 9.

If this passage is viewed within the context of the overall framework of *2 Baruch*, it is necessary to acknowledge that the author seeks to speak to the whole people of Israel, although he does so by recourse to apocalyptic themes and literary devices. One might, therefore, conclude that the same prophetic theory of divine wisdom is at work in both Daniel 9 and *2 Baruch* 4.

II

It is necessary to point out that there is a basic difference between such a theory operating within the context of prophetic inspiration and the application of the same theory to the broader field of biblical interpretation. Ordinary people would not dispute the prophet's access to heavenly secrets. Job 15.8 could be taken as an illustration of this. Eliphaz reminds Job of his own limits: 'Have you listened to the council of God? And do you limit wisdom to yourself?' The obvious answer is a negative one, and so Eliphaz concludes, 'for your iniquity teaches your mouth and you choose the tongue of the crafty' (Job 15.5). In other words, Job cannot lay claim to any knowledge of heavenly things, nor to understanding and experience beyond that available to all (compare Job 15.9-10).

Interpretation of Scripture falls most naturally into this category of human understanding and experience. By its very nature, Scripture and its interpretation should be accessible to the public. The Bible itself provides a most illuminating account of the public reading of the

1. For this text see I. Grünwald, 'From Rise to Dawn: Forms of Jewish Eschatology and Messianism' (Hebrew), in *The Messianic Idea in Jewish Thought: A Study Conference in Honour of G. Scholem* (Jerusalem, 1990), pp. 18-36, esp. pp. 28-29.

'book of the law of Moses, which the LORD had given to Israel' (Neh. 8.1). It is disputed as to whether this incident marks the introduction of the Pentateuch, as we have it now, as sacred Scripture. Nevertheless, the event described in the book of Nehemiah involves a public reading of the 'law of Moses' (8.2) to 'both men and women and all who could hear with understanding' (8.2-3). Verse 8 stresses, 'so they read from the book, from the law of God, with interpretation. They gave the sense, so that the people understood the reading'. That is, the reading took place in public and was accompanied by an explanation of its meaning: interpretation necessarily accompanies the reading of a text. Those who wish to keep a religious tradition as the exclusive property of an elite cannot do so once the central text is accessible to the public. This is precisely the point being made in Nehemiah 8: the law is now read before virtually the entire people.

Such a text is totally different from prophetic utterances which are bound to the person of this or that prophet, his imagination and claims of contact with the divine. Nevertheless, prophets may use and interpret other traditions known to the public. It is important to differentiate between a text open to public interpretation and a particular prophetic speech, built as it is upon the intimate relationship between this outstanding individual and the Deity.

On the basis of the two texts discussed, it would seem legitimate to suggest that apocalypticism develops this distinction: in both cases the interpreted scriptural verses are drawn from prophetic writings. However, other apocalyptic writings can also interpret the Law. Some interpretations will serve to illuminate the apocalypticists' claim to be the bearers of a 'second revelation'. However, at this point, it should be noted that the combination of the prophetic tradition of direct access to the divine and the quest for legitimate interpretation of Scripture deprives Scripture of its public openness. The result is that the right to interpret the text (and the right to apply its meaning) is restricted to a minority group or elite.

The development under discussion, at least in the period of the Second Jewish Commonwealth, is deeply connected with apocalyptic circles. Other interpretations of Scripture also emerged in this period. The scale of rewritten Scripture reaches from 1 and 2 Chronicles to Pseudo-Philo's *Liber Antiquitarum Biblicarum*. However, in these rewritings of Scripture no claim is made to divine revelation. The close connection between interpretation and revelation is primarily characteristic of apocalypticism and the Jewish sects which adopted this worldview. This fact bears directly upon the question under discussion and is a point to which I shall return.

III

Within the literary corpus associated with the apocalyptic worldview, the book of *Jubilees* stands out for a number of reasons.[1] Normally dated in the second century BCE, it is one of the few writings in this genre which deals with religious law (halakha).[2] Fictionally, the prescriptions are related to the praxis of the patriarchs; in actual fact, they are taken over from the biblical account or interpret it. In order to relate his new interpretations to the biblical story, the author rewrites the book of Genesis and the opening sections of Exodus. However, in contrast to other works of this period he appeals to angelic mediation: the new book is dictated to Moses by the Angel of Presence. This 'dictation' is presented as a continuation of Moses' dialogue with God on Mount Sinai, that is, it is given at the same time as the written Law.

The book of *Jubilees* is not just another book, but rather interpretation of the earlier texts.[3] Having said this, it was not intended as a replacement for the earlier Law. From time to time, the author refers to the 'first book which I entrusted to you'.[4] In other words, he accepts the authority of that first book as binding and strives to show that his own account conforms with Mosaic Law. Yet, at the same time, the author is conscious that he is in fact rewriting existing Scripture. It seems reasonable to suggest that the claim to angelic revelation is a device which serves to legitimate the author's own

1. This formulation tries to do some justice to the fact that not every apocalyptic writing is an 'apocalypse' by the definition of this literary genre.

2. The basic study for *Jubilees*' derivations from biblical law as understood by the later Jewish sages remains C. Albeck, *Das Buch der Jubiläen und die Halacha* (Bericht der Hochschule fur die Wissenschaft des Judentums, 46; Berlin, 1930).

3. It is astonishing that J.C. Endres' book *Biblical Interpretation in the Book of Jubilees* (CBQMS, 18; Washington, DC: Catholic Biblical Association, 1987) deals with the question posed here only in an epilogue; see pp. 249ff. I am unable to follow G.L. Davenport's thesis that 'the author of the discourse did not intend to interpret the Pentateuch, but to draw upon it for the ancestral history...' See his *The Eschatology of the Book of Jubilees* (SPB, 20; Leiden: Brill, 1970), p. 11 n. 7.

4. To *Jub.* 1.26, cf. 6.22; 30.12-21; 50.6.

'second' revelation, and thus also the unorthodox religious praxis of his community. The general tendency in such interpretations is to urge Israel into a more clear-cut separation from the Gentiles.[1] In other words, the theological compulsion to regard separation as a binding commandment leads the author to interpret the religious Law in such a way that it is formulated as a new, or 'second', revelation. Or, more precisely, the author's own interpretation is presented as a second aspect of the one original and binding revelation given on Mount Sinai.

It is not known whether or not such halakhic prescriptions were ever practised. The book of *Jubilees* was found among the remains of the Qumran library. This community left the rest of the people and settled in the wilderness in order to live there according to its understanding of the tradition. It is here that we find a developed theory of Scripture interpretation by reference to what might be called a 'second revelation'. The locus classicus in this respect is 1QpHab.[2] This text belongs to a group of *pesharim*, commentaries on biblical texts (mostly prophetic writings) which aim at an actualization.[3] However, 1QpHab 7.5 maintains that the interpretation of Habakkuk's

1.   See especially E. Schwarz, *Identität durch Abgrenzung: Abgrenzungsprozesse in Israel im 2. vorchristlichen Jahrhundert und ihre traditionsgeschichtlichen Voraussetzungen: Zugleich ein Beitrag zur Erforschung des Jubiläenbuches* (Europäische Hochschulschriften, 23.162; Frankfurt am Main, 1982).

2.   This text does not stand alone. It simply highlights that conception in the Qumran literature, as indeed the Qumranites saw themselves to be in contact with the angels, not only as single devotees but as a group. This is not the place to deal with this aspect of Qumranite theology. The history of the *terminus technicus* פשר directs us towards an esoteric understanding; see F. Bruce, *Biblical Exegesis in the Qumran Texts* (Exegetica, 3.1; The Hague, 1959), pp. 7ff., 14ff.; for further explanations of the terms רז, סוד etc. see also M. Küchler, *Frühjüdische Weisheitstraditionen: Zum Fortgang weisheitlichen Denkens im Bereich des frühjüdischen Jahweglaubens* (OBO, 26; Freiburg, 1979), pp. 92-100; for the difference between this attitude and that of Daniel, see Fishbane, *Biblical Interpretation*, pp. 509ff.

3.   See M.P. Horgan, *Pesharim: Qumran Interpretations of Biblical Books* (CBQMS, 8; Washington DC, 1979); and recently H. Feltes, *die Gattung des Habakukkommentars von Qumran (1QpHab): Eine Studie zum frühen jüdischen Midrash* (Forschungen zur Bibel, 58; Würzburg, 1986). Feltes discusses the problem of a 'second revelation' on pp. 173-91 (see there for further literature). However, his own view is not really clear.

prophecy was revealed to the Teacher of Righteousness: ואשר אמר למען
ירוץ הקורא בו פשרו על מורה הצדק אשר הודיעו אל את כול רזי דברי עבדיו
הנביאים ('And regarding that which he said, *'that he who reads it may
read speedily* [Hab. 2.2], the interpretation of this concerns the
Teacher of Righteousness, to whom God made known all the mysteries of the words of his servants the prophets').[1]

In other words, the prophecy of Habakkuk stems from God, but for
an exact interpretation a 'second revelation' is required. Most commentators suggest that this kind of actualization takes place in Qumran
literature because the Qumranites expected the end of the world in the
near future. Yet Betz[2] has already shown that there are other factors
to be considered, most notably the right understanding of the legal
practices laid down in the Law, that is the Pentateuch.[3]

It is clear that the 'Teacher of Righteousness' was opposed to a
religious establishment which, in the Qumran texts, is most often
identified with the 'wicked priest'. Although we do not know the
identity of those involved, the conflict as such is particularly illuminating in the context of our present discussion: the prophetic claim to
divine wisdom is made on behalf of the 'Teacher' of the Qumran
community in the context of the struggle against another application
of the Jewish Law to a specific historic situation.

The position taken in Qumran is similar to that adopted in the book
of *Jubilees*; that is, an unorthodox religious praxis is legitimated by
reference to a particular interpretation of Scripture, itself grounded in
an appeal to a new or 'second' revelation. This approach is thus
grounded in a community's need to justify its particular interpretation
of the prescriptions of the Law. However, the implications of this
approach go much further.

---

1. The Hebrew text is quoted according to the edition of B. Nitzan, *Pesher
Habakkuk: A Scroll from the Wilderness of Judaea (1QpHab): Text, Introduction
and Commentary* (Jerusalem, 1986), p. 171. See also pp. 156ff.

2. See O. Betz, *Offenbarung un Schriftforschung in der Qumransekte* (WUNT,
6; Tübingen: Mohr [Paul Siebeck], 1960), pp. 6ff., as well as Blenkinsopp,
'Interpretation and Sectarianism', n. 116.

3. Blenkinsopp wishes to interpret some of the texts involved as intending the
special Qumran laws; see 'Interpretation and Sectarianism', p. 23. However, this
distinction loses its importance once the sectarian law is presented as the 'true'
interpretation of the Pentateuch, as Blenkinsopp himself makes clear.

Before discussing these further implications, it would be helpful to consider another text that takes up this new developed theory of interpretation. The text I have in mind is *2 Enoch*. The book can easily be divided into three parts. The first tells of Enoch's ascension to heaven.[1] The second describes his audience before the throne of God, and the third contains Enoch's ethical instructions to his sons, given in the last years of his life.[2] This structure clearly indicates that the ethical instructions are a result of the divine speech in the second part in the light of Enoch's approaching death. Viewed in this context, the contents of the divine speech are astonishing: God tells Enoch the creation story up to Adam and Eve's expulsion from Paradise (*2 En.* 24.2-32). The divine interpretation of Scripture thus prepares the way for the subsequent ethical instruction. This, therefore, is to be understood as the true substance of the creation story. One particular detail of this story is instructive: the date of God's revelation to Enoch is given as the sixth of Sivan (the same day was both Enoch's birthday and the date of his death [68.13J]), that is, the date of the Jewish Feast of Weeks which, in turn, was traditionally associated with the revelation at Sinai.[3] It is hardly likely that this choice of date was accidental. It seems more probable that a parallel is being drawn between the creation story and the revelation of the Law on Sinai.

2 Enoch, therefore, does not fit into the same framework of a struggle over the interpretation of the Law.[4] Thus, this example of the

1.   The unexpected change of the number of heavens from seven to ten cannot be discussed here.

2.   There is still no convincing solution regarding the fourth part, the story about Melchizidek's miraculous birth (which is not extant in some manuscripts). The question has no bearing upon my discussion.

3.   The longer version reads: 'and he [Enoch] was taken up into heaven [in the month] Nissan, on the first day. And he remained in heaven for 60 days writing down all [those] notes about the creatures which the Lord had created. And he wrote 366 books and handed them over to his sons, and he remained on the earth for 30 days, talking with them, and then he was taken up into heaven again in the month of Sivan on the 6th day, on the very 6th day which he was ever born and at the very same hour'.

4.   However, it should be asked here whether or not this apocalypse really belongs to the Jewish stream of apocalyptic thought. The concluding section about the miraculous birth of Melchizedek allows at least for an interpretation within Christian apocalypticism, which nevertheless might have used some Jewish elements. But it seems inappropriate to accept the whole book as a Jewish

divine retelling of Scripture would appear to support Grünwald's view that there are a number of other implications contained in revealed and rewritten Scripture, most notably esoteric ones.[1]

We know of other accounts of revelation within apocalyptic literature and these are sometimes connected to the revelation of the Law to Moses.[2] However, these additional apocalyptic sources do not retell the content of Scripture but relate specifically to a particular book (or books). On the other hand, as I have already indicated, interpretations of Scripture not given in an apocalyptic framework, such as Pseudo-Philo's *Liber Antiquarum Biblicarum* and others, lack the claim of a special 'second revelation'. Yet the connection between this theory and apocalypticism provides the key to understanding its sociological importance.

IV

The development I have traced is rooted in a sociological context, yet also contributes to a new sociological reality. It is therefore necessary to address the nature of this 'reality'. What, precisely, do we know about it? In the end it seems fair to conclude that we are confronted with the mythological expression of a socio-religious truth, the true meaning of which only becomes apparent years later with the development of a more sophisticated philosophical language. I would like now to take up these issues, albeit briefly.

The roots of the apocalyptic movement are located in the profound changes that took place during the Second Temple period.[3] Apocalypticism, as a national religious movement during the greater

composition. Be that as it may, the role of Scripture interpretation in this work is an outstanding one.

1. See Grünwald, *Apocalyptic and Merkavah Mysticism*, 'Two Types of Jewish Esoteric Literature', and *From Apocalypticism to Gnosticism*.

2. The 24 books which Ezra is allowed to publish, according to *4 Ezra* 12.42-47, are normally identified as the Jewish canon of Scripture; likewise, it appears that the *scripturae* and *libri* mentioned in *Ass. Mos.* 1.15-17 belong to the same category; see the commentary by A. Schalit, *Unterschungen zur Assumptio Mosis* (Arbeiten zu Literatur und Geschichte des hellenistischen Judentums, 17; Leiden, 1989), pp. 154-208, especially pp. 178-80.

3. Insofar as this is a 'movement'! We have no information about most of the individuals who took part in the formation of this literature. With regard to the Qumran community, the unknown outweighs the known.

part of this epoch, is an expression of the ideas of a minority, but a minority which defined itself as a distinctive group in contrast to the majority.[1] The author of the *Similitudes of Enoch* refers to the righteous ones as 'the elect'. There is no doubt as to the Jewish identity of this 'elect'. However, simply being Jewish is not in itself sufficient grounds for membership of this particular group. To quote Grünwald, 'the apocalypticists define themselves as the chosen ones within the "chosen" People'.[2] The location of the Qumran community in the Judaean desert provides the strongest evidence for this particular group's separation from the rest of Israel. *Jubilees* lays out a whole series of prescriptions and regulations with the aim of preserving Israel's self-imposed isolation.[3] It is illuminating to observe the change of attitude in apocalyptic writings after the fall of the Second Temple: the authors of *4 Ezra* and *2 Baruch* are deeply concerned with the fate of this minority throughout. Salvation is promised to 'you and those like you'; in other words, both authors still maintain that only a part of Israel will be saved. Yet these two authors then start to question why this is so. We may conclude, then, that apocalypticism is a kind of inner emigration, a self-imposed exile from the rest of the community on the basis of an elitist understanding of the self as one of the 'elect'. This emigration indicates a deep shift within Jewish society. What brought about this shift? The majority of apocalyptic writings are strongly opposed to the Jerusalem Temple and its cult, rather than to sacrifices per se. More than this, apocalypticism has a well-formulated theory of the salvation of the poor. Apocalyptic writers often warn the rich and the governing class of the judgment awaiting them on 'that day', that is, the day of judgment. In the period of the Second Jewish Commonwealth this class was closely connected with the religious establishment, and the personal union of the high priest and the Jewish king is no more than an outstanding

1.   This despite the possibility that apocalyptic motifs and motives may have played an essential role in the self definition of the Jewish revolutionaries in the last days of the Second Temple. This possibility is a strong one and it is, at least indirectly, confirmed by Josephus. See M. Hengel, *The Zealots: Investigations into the Jewish Freedom Movement in the Period from Herod I until 70 AD* (Edinburgh: T.&T. Clark, 1989). We should consider, then, the growing significance of this *Weltanschaung* towards the end of the period.

2.   Personal communication.

3.   See Schwarz, *Identität durch Abgrenzung*, n. 13.

symbol of this connection. Yet the ongoing shift between rich and poor in Israel in that time has been an often repeated sociological phenomenon. It should be added that the governing class has been closely associated with Hellenistic culture and the foreign rulers over the country.

Such a context may explain the apocalypticist's need for a new revelation in the face of the religious and temporal authorities. The newly made claim of access to heavenly wisdom is adopted from prophetic literature, which includes numerous prophecies against foreign rulers, the rich and even the Temple and its cult. However, in the apocalyptic writings of the Second Temple period, the priestly element becomes more prominent than in earlier prophetic writing.[1] Such a development might suggest priestly involvement in such writing.

Yet, at the same time, the return to prophetic patterns of legitimation suggests another sociological reality: not every member of the group is likely to have the same encounter with the Deity, to have access to the heavenly council. This means that the appeal to prophetic patterns of legitimation is likely to result in a new hierarchy within the apocalyptic group. The role played by the 'Teacher of Righteousness' within the Qumran community serves to illustrate the point. Most scholars would accept this view.[2]

However, there are still some questions to be settled. Given the outstanding role of *2 Enoch*, including the divine retelling of Genesis 1–3, as well as the more general tradition of heavenly journeys and the revelations granted to the apocalypticist as a consequence of these, the position outlined above does not serve to explain all the relevant texts. Our knowledge of this period and the individuals involved is too scanty to draw overall conclusions. Moreover, the organization of apocalyptic groups, other than the Qumran community, is by no means fully known to us. In effect, we know only that apocalyptic

---

1.   For the background of the following observations see especially I. Grünwald, 'The Impact of Priestly Traditions on the Creation of Merkabah Mysticism and the Shiur Komah' (Hebrew), in *Proceedings of the First International Conference on the History of Jewish Mysticism: Early Jewish Mysticism* (Jerusalem Studies in Jewish Thought, 6.1-2; Jerusalem, 1987), pp. 65-120; D. Suter, 'Fallen Angel, Fallen Priest: The Problem of Family Purity in 1 Enoch 6-16', *HUCA* 50 (1979), pp. 115-35.

2.   See the previous note, and cf. for example Bruce, *Biblical Exegesis*, p. 18: 'Many a religious minority will venerate a Teacher of Righteousness...'

literature often speaks of the 'elect'. However, one must bear in mind
that religious divergences brought about the formation of different
groups, and vice versa. It is clear today that every group constitutes
itself by, among other means, formulating some laws to govern its
own existence. It seems only natural that Jews should do this by reference to some acknowledged Scripture. How far did such different
views lead to the formation of new groups within Judaism, and how
far did the emergence of new groups within Judaism result in the
creation of new codes of practice? Given the current extent of our
knowledge of the period, there is no answer to this question.
Nevertheless, one should bear in mind the possibility that some of the
formulated divergences are nothing less than the theoretical formulations of a group's internal laws.

I raised the question of the legitimacy of diverse apocalyptic interpretations. Apocalypticists, such as the author of the book of Daniel,
responded to the question of the legitimacy of their new interpretation
of older Scripture by appealing to what could be described as a
prophetic claim to revelation. Interpretations of Scripture are not, in
such cases, judged by means of logic or rules of hermeneutics. Rather,
the writers invoke 'mythological' language which speaks of angelic
visits (as in Dan. 9.21) and other similar modes of divine revelation.
To reflect upon this phenomenon sociologically, it clearly has a tendency towards sectarianism, given that only members of the same
religious group, that is, those who interpret Scripture in a similar
way, will be able to perceive the 'truth' of the apocalypticist's message.[1] We might say, in cases such as Daniel 9, that scriptural interpretation is to be understood in terms of the self-definition of the
interpreting community, even when such interpretation is couched in
what we might consider to be 'mythological' language. Different
religious communities may use the same sacred Scripture but apply it
in different ways. If this is taken seriously, perhaps the question of the
'right' or 'legitimate' interpretation is not the most appropriate one.

The phenomenon which I have described as 'second revelation',
divinely inspired exegesis, was to play a fundamental part in both
early Christian and rabbinic interpretation. However, it is interesting
to note that, whereas in the cases previously discussed the group

---

1. A possible modern parallel could be found in Karl Barth's emphasis on the
dependence of human interpretation on divine revelation. See his interpretation of
Proslogion (Fides Quaerens Intellectum; Zürich: Theologischer Verlag, 1981).

engaged in interpreting Scripture remained a sect, in these latter cases we are dealing with 'sects' which emerged as the mainstream or majority. The way in which the phenomenon of 'second revelation' functions in developed mainstream communities is a further question and best left for another occasion.

Bavli versus Bible: System and Imputed Tradition versus Tradition and Imputed System

Jacob Neusner

One way in which intellectuals reframe received writings into a
single, systematic statement is to adopt the commentary form for the
presentation of what is, in fact, a quite independent statement of their
own. This imputes to that statement the standing of tradition, cloaking
with the garment of tradition something that in fact sets forth a quite
new message. This is true of the Talmud of Babylonia, or Bavli,
which is the foundation document of Judaism, produced in the seventh
century. This document, anonymous and authoritative, a social document rather than a private one, was set forth as a commentary on the
Mishnah and on Scripture alike; but in it its writers made their
coherent and independent statement upon the entire received corpus
and restated it in the manner of their own choice. The independent act
of selecting passages requiring comment created a principal intellectual labour of system-building. In the case of the Christian mind,
where do we look for a counterpart labour of system-building
through selectivity? The answer, of course, is dictated by the question.
We turn to the work of canonization of available writings into the
Bible. There we see the counterpart, the making of choices, the setting
forth of a single statement. When we compare the systemic structures
represented by the Bavli and the Bible, therefore, we can appreciate
how two quite distinct groups of intellectuals worked out solutions to
a single problem, and did so, as a matter of fact, through pretty much
the same medium, namely, the making of reasoned choices.

The Bavli's was not the only solution to the problem of cultural
continuity within a cogent community, because imputing the standing
of tradition to what was in fact an original and fresh system has an
opposite. That is to gather together traditions and to impose upon
them the form and structure of a system. And that is the method of

holding things together in a stable composite that Christian intellectuals of the second and third centuries found in their quest to extract,
out of writings deemed authoritative a single Christian truth, that is to
say, what we should call a system.

The comparison of the way of the Bavli to the manner of the Bible
is apt not only because both led to a solution of the perennial problem
of an ongoing society facing the advent of the permanently-new.
There is a second reason to undertake precisely the comparison before
us. It is the simple fact that, in the study of the formation of the
Jewish intellect within the history of Judaism, the ineluctable source of
comparisons derives from Christianity, because all Judaic and
Christian systems appeal to the same originating Scriptures held
authoritative or holy, namely, the Written Torah for the Judaism of
the Dual Torah, the Old Testament for all Orthodox and Catholic
Christianity. They commonly do so, moreover, in pretty much the
same way, that is to say, by quoting verses of ancient Israel's
Scripture as prooftexts for their respective propositions. Implicit is
the same position, that the (selected) Scripture of ancient Israel bore
probative authority in disposing of claims of the faith.[1] And that
simple fact further defines the point of comparison. To specify what I
deem comparable in the two traditions, I point to the simple fact that
each defines its authority by appeal to revelation, and both religious
traditions know precisely the locus of revelation.

The comparison at hand may be simply stated. The Bible, for
Christianity, and the Bavli, for Judaism, have not only formed the
court of final appeal in issues of doctrine and (for Judaism) normative
instruction on correct deeds. Each writing in its way has solved for its
family of religious systems a fundamental dilemma of intellect and
culture. But, while the comparison is not only justified but demanded,
still the Bavli and the Bible present us with quite different kinds of
documents. And in the differences we see the choices people made
when confronting pretty much the same problem. For in late
antiquity, from the second through the fourth centuries for Orthodox

---

1. The Islamic appeal to the Old Testament/Written Torah requires attention on
its own terms. I am not qualified to undertake the comparison of the use of that
ancient Scripture in the Quran and later Islamic writings, nor to suggest how that use
compares with and contrast to the Judaic and Christian use of the same writings. In
this respect, however, I do think that there is a 'Judaeo–Christian' tradition, but it is,
of course, one that divides, and not unites, the Judaic and Christian religions.

and Catholic Christianity and from the second through the seventh centuries for the Judaism of the Dual Torah, the Judaic and Christian intellectuals sorted out the complex problem of relating the worlds of the then-moderns to the words of the ancients. Both groups of intellectuals then claimed to present enduring traditions, a fundament of truth revealed of old. But both sets of thinkers also brought to realization systematic and philosophical statements, which begin in first principles and rise in steady and inexorable logic to final conclusions: compositions of proportion, balance, cogency and order.

Christianity finds in the Bible (by which I mean the Old Testament and the New Testament) the statement of the faith by authority of God.[1] And however diverse the readings of the Bible, Christian theologians, Catholic (Roman or Greek or Armenian or Russian in language) and Protestant alike define the foundations of all divine knowledge as the simple fact that there is a pattern of Christian truth, awaiting discovery and demonstration. So all Christianities appeal not to diverse traditions, insusceptible of harmonization, but to a Christian truth, the idea of orthodoxy, if not to the same Orthodoxy. Accordingly Christianities concur that there is more than tradition, there is also what we should call system, one Christian system, whatever it may be. And the Bible forms the statement of that system, however we choose to read it. Accordingly, the Bible for all Christianities forms traditions into a single system.

For its part, the regnant Judaism from antiquity to our own day, the Judaism of the Dual Torah, presents itself not as an invented system of the sixth century, elaborated, adapted, expanded, revised from then to now, but as tradition, specifically, the increment of truth revealed by God to Moses and handed on, generation by generation, with each generation contributing to the sedimentary legacy of Sinai. And that Judaism has identified in the Bavli, the Talmud of Babylonia, the summa of the Torah of Sinai, joining as it does the Written Torah, encompassing what Christianity knows as the Old Testament, and the Oral Torah, commencing with the Mishnah. The systematic character of the statement of the Bavli, the cogency of its logic and its systemic statement, the paramount and blatant character of its self-evidently

---

1.   It is not pertinent to deal with tradition as a correlative source of God's truth, and I take no position on the controversial issues of Christianity as to whether solely Scripture, or Scripture and also tradition preserved by the teaching authority of the church, constitute the authoritative repository of revelation.

valid answer to its sustaining and critical question—these facts require no elaboration. It suffices only to repeat that the Bavli represents system as tradition. Comparison also requires observation of contrasts, and, as a matter of fact, the points of difference are determined by the shared morphology: the Bible and the Bavli are very different ways of setting forth a system. Each represents its components in a distinctive manner, the one by preserving their autonomy and calling the whole a system, the other by obscuring their originally autonomous and independent character and imparting to the whole the form of tradition. The upshot may be simply stated. The Bavli presents a system and imputes to it, through the operative logics, the standing of tradition. The Bible sets forth diverse and unsystematic traditions, received writings from we know not where, and to those traditions, through the act of canonization, imputes the character and structure of (a) system.

To unpack these generalizations, let us turn back to the literary media in which the intellects of the two communities set forth their system as traditions or their traditions as system: the Bavli and the Bible, respectively. We wish specifically to see how each of these monuments of mind works out its own system and, consequently, accomplishes the tasks at hand: first, choosing a logic of cogent discourse to serve the interests of the system, and secondly, situating the system in relationship to received and authoritative, prior systemic statements.

In the case of the Bavli, I call attention to the odd mixture of logics utilized by the framers of the system as a whole. On the one side, sentences were formed into coherent statements through the normal logic of proposition and syllogism, to which we are all accustomed. On the other, groups of sentences—paragraphs—were linked only to a prior text, the Mishnah itself; and this is not a propositional mode of coherent discourse, but one I call 'discourse that coheres through the logic of fixed association'. So we may ask, why did the composers of the Bavli find it necessary to resort to that mixture?

The Bavli's framers wished to present a system in the disguise of a tradition, and hence set a high priority upon relating their ideas to received writings. But when they read the Mishnah, they found a writing with a quite opposite intent, which was, as we remember, to appeal for power of persuasion not to (mere) authority but to the compelling force of logic, structure and order. When we understand the character of the Mishnah and its relationship to the immediately prior system its authorship recognized, the Pentateuch (and Scripture as a whole), we shall grasp the choices confronting the Bavli's[1] framers. The issue then was authority, and the position of the authorship of one system simply contradicted the datum of the authorship of the successor-system. What the Bavli's framers did, then, was to subvert the received system by imposing upon it precisely the character the Mishnah's authorship had rejected, namely, that of a commentary to Scripture, a secondary expansion of Scripture. And—it would inexorably follow—the Bavli's framers then adopted for their own system that same form that they again and again imposed upon the Mishnah's system.[2]

When we come to the counterpart religious world, we confront Christian intellectuals (dealing also with the inheritance of ancient Israel's Scriptures) facing the same problem. The parallel is exact in yet another aspect. Just as the authorship of the Bavli received not only what they came to call the Written Torah but also the Mishnah and other writings that had attained acceptance, hence authority, from the closure of the Mishnah to their own day, so too did the Christian intellectuals inherit more than the Old Testament. They too had in hand a variety of authoritative documents, to which the inspiration of the Holy Spirit was imputed. So they confronted the same problem as faced the authorship of the Bavli, and it was in pretty much the same terms: namely, how to sort out received documents, each of which made its own statement,[3] took up a different problem and followed a different solution to that problem. The issue of the authority of contradictory traditions defined the task at hand.

What the Christian intellectuals did, working over several centuries from c. 100 through c. 400, was to join together the received writings as autonomous books but to impute to the whole the standing of a

1.   And the Yerushalmi's.
2.   Thus as a matter of fact obliterating the Mishnah's system altogether.
3.   Whether that is a systemic statement or not, and for the present purpose, the analysis of systemic compositions and constructions within the Christian framework is not required. My purpose is solely to place in relationship two solutions to the problem of system and tradition. While an analysis of the systemic traits of Christian writing down to the canonization of the (Christian) Bible (the Old Testament and the New Testament) would prove extremely suggestive, it has not been done, and I cannot pretend to be able to do it.

cogent statement, a single and harmonious Christian truth. This they did in the work of making the biblical canon,[1] joining diverse traditions into one uniform and, therefore (putatively) harmonious Bible: God's word. And, once more, this explains my view that the Christian solution to the problem of making a statement but also situating that system in relationship to received tradition is to be characterized as imputing system to discrete traditions through a declared canon. Thus, as in the title of this essay, the comparison of the solutions that would prevail, respectively, in Judaism's Bavli and Christianity's Bible are characterized as a system to which the standing of tradition is imputed, as against traditions to which the form of a single system is, through the canonization of scriptures as the Bible, imputed.[2]

The legitimacy of my comparing the two intellects through their ultimate statements, the Bavli and the Bible, seems to me sustained by the simple theological judgment of H.E.W. Turner: 'The mind of the Church [in making the canon] was guided by criteria rationally devised and flexibly applied. There is no dead hand in the production of the Canon; there is rather the living action of the Holy Spirit using as He is wont the full range of the continuing life of the Church to achieve His purposes in due season'.[3] I can find no better language to state, in a way interior to a system, the claim that a writing or a set of writings constitutes a system: a way of life, a worldview, an address to

1.   I hasten to add that they did so not only in the process of the canonization of some writings as the Old Testament and the New Testament, the Bible. It seems to me that the work of framing creeds, preparing liturgies to be used throughout the church(es), debating theology and the like all attended to the same labour of stating the pattern of Christian truth out of the received writings, all of them claiming to be derived from the Holy Spirit or to be consonant with writings that did, that competed for standing and that contradicted one another on pretty much every important point. Once more, I underline that in dealing only with the work of canon, I in no way pretend to address the broader issues implicit in the topic as I have defined it.

2.   In laying matters out, I avoid entering the issues debated in R.A. Kraft and G. Krodel (eds.), *Orthodoxy and Heresy in Earliest Christianity* (trans. W. Bauer; Philadelphia: Fortress Press, 1971; originally published in German as *Rechtglaubigkeit und Ketzerei im ältesten Christentum* [1934, supplemented by G. Strecker, 1964]), and H.E.W. Turner, *The Pattern of Christian Truth: A Study of the Relations Between Orthodoxy and Heresy in the Early Church (The Bampton Lectures, 1954)* (London: A.R. Mowbray & Co., 1954). I do claim that my representation of matters accords with Turner's chapter 'Orthodoxy and the Bible', pp. 241ff.

3.   Turner, *Pattern of Christian Truth*, p. 258.

a particular social entity. This too is made explicit by Turner, who I take to be a thoroughly reliable representative of Christian theology on the subject:

> There can be no doubt that the Bible is fundamentally an orthodox book, sufficient if its teaching is studied as a whole to lead to orthodox conclusions. . . The Biblical data insist upon arranging themselves in certain theological patterns and cannot be forced into other moulds without violent distortion. That is the point of a famous simile of St Irenaeus. The teaching of Scripture can be compared to a mosaic of the head of a king, but the heretics break up the pattern and reassemble it in the form of a dog or a fox.[1]

A master of the Bavli could not have said it better in claiming both the systemic character and the traditional standing of his statement.

Let me hasten to qualify the comparison at hand. In claiming that a single problem, one of relating a system to tradition, for Judaism, or traditions into a system, for Christianity, found two solutions in the Bavli and the Bible respectively, I do not for one minute suggest that the two groups of intellectuals were thinking along the same lines at all. Quite on the contrary, the comparison derives from a different standpoint altogether. For, if we ask, when the Christian theologians worked out the idea of 'the Bible'—consisting of 'the Old Testament and the New Testament'—and when the Judaic theologians worked out the idea of 'the Dual Torah'—consisting of 'the Written Torah and the Oral Torah'—did each group propose to answer a question also confronting the other group, we answer in the negative. For, as a matter of fact, each party pursued a problem particular to the internal logic and life of its own group. They were different people talking about the same thing to different people. It is true that, as a matter of necessity, each party had to designate within the larger corpus of scriptures deriving from ancient Israel those writings that it regarded as authoritative and therefore divinely revealed. But did the one side do so for the same reasons, and within the same sort of theological logic, that the other did? Each party had further to explain to itself the end-result, that is, the revealed words as a whole. What are they all together, all at once? The one party characterized the whole as a single Bible, book, piece of writing, and the other party characterized the whole as a single Torah, revelation, in two media, the one writing,

---

1. Turner, *Pattern of Christian Truth*, p. 300.

the other memory. But these characterizations of the result of revelation, that is, of the canon, hardly constitute intersecting statements. The reason that, for Christianity, traditions become a system, as Turner testifies was the intent and the outcome, derives from the life of the church, not from the issues of culture in its relationship to change, or of system in its realization in the logic of cogent discourse, such as I have framed here.

This is indeed what makes the matter so intensely interesting even now, namely the capacity of rigorously disciplined theologians to state in terms of their language and the compelling logic particular to their intellects what we for our part perceive as not logical at all, but as (merely) adventitious perplexities of the ongoing social world of culture. That is to say, in simple language, things happen. People write books. Other people believe in those books. There need not be a logic to form from those diverse writings a single harmonious statement, a system, a stunning answer to an ineluctable question. But the Christian theologians took a sizeable corpus of unrelated documents and turned them into the Bible, and they furthermore imputed to that Bible the character of a system and even claimed to uncover, within the Bible, structure, order, proportion, harmony and, by the way, doctrine, hence Christian truth. And the Judaic sages did no less, but they did it with different kinds of writings, for different reasons, and in a different way. The issue framed as discovering the pattern of Christian truth addressed the authority of received writings and their harmony, and that issue, I maintain, faced the Judaic sages in their encounter with the system of the Mishnah. But for both Christian and Judaic intellectuals, the issues at hand derived from the very nature of the social world, its continuing to evolve in patterns not imposed by the logic of an inherited system, but determined only by the inexorable but immediate confrontation of the latest generation with the questions imposed upon it by the advent of a fresh tomorrow.[1]

We began with a labour of comparison. We do well to remind ourselves that we compare things that are really not like one another. For we now realize that the issues important to the Judaism of the sages were in no way consubstantial with the issues at hand. None of the cited theological precipitants for the canonical process in a Judaic

1. And that, if I may say so, is what makes the study of the history of religions as intensely contemporary as I find it to be. But that is a separate question.

formulation played any role I can discern in the theory of the Torah in two media. The myth of the Dual Torah, which functioned as a canonical process, validating as it did the writings of sages as part of Torah from Sinai, derives from neither the analogy to the Old Testament process nor—to begin with—from the narrow issue of finding a place for the specific writings of rabbis within the larger Torah; and, it follows, we cannot refer to 'the Bible' when we speak of Judaism.[1] When scholars of the formation of the canon of Christianity use the word canon, they mean, first, the recognition of sacred Scripture, over and beyond the (received) Hebrew Scriptures; secondly, the identification of writings revered within the church as canonical, hence authoritative; thirdly, the recognition that these accepted writings formed a Scripture, which, fourthly, served as the counterpart to the Hebrew Scriptures; hence, fifthly, the formation of the Bible as the Old and New Testaments. Now, as a matter of fact, none of these categories, stage by stage, corresponds in any way to the processes in the unfolding of the holy books of the sages, which I shall now describe in terms of Torah. But the word 'Torah' in the context of the writings of the sages at hand in no way forms that counterpart to the word 'canon' as used (quite correctly) by Childs,[2] von Campenhausen[3] and others, and moreover the word 'Bible' and the word 'Torah' in no way speak of the same thing, that is, they do not refer to the same category or classification.

But the difference is the very point of the comparison, for, after all, the generative problematic was the same: holding together received conceptions in a contemporary statement, answering new questions out of inherited truths, setting forth a system in such a way as to affirm its traditional authority (Judaism), setting forth tradition in such a way as to claim its systemic harmony (Christianity). So the differences require underlining. And this requires a set of banal observations. First, the statement of the Bavli is not a canonical system at all. In the

1.   To state the simple fact, first comes the explanation of the place and role of the sage and his teachings, then comes the explanation of the place of the books that contain those teachings—in that order. I do not mean to ignore interesting debates on the canonization of the Christian Bible, meaning the Old and the New Testaments.

2.   B.S. Childs, *Myth and Reality in the Old Testament* (London: SCM Press, 1962).

3.   H. von Campenhausen, *The Formation of the Christian Bible* (trans. J.A. Baker; London: A. & C. Black, 1972).

mode of presentation of the Bavli's system, as a matter of fact, revelation does not close or reach conclusion. God speaks all the time, through the sages. Representing the whole as 'Torah' means that the Bavli speaks a tradition formed in God's revelation of God's will to Moses, our rabbi. Ancient Israel's Scriptures fall into the category of Torah, but they do not fill that category up. Other writings fall into that same category. 'Torah' refers to various things that fall into a particular classification, while by contrast 'canon' refers to particular books that enjoy a distinctive standing. There is a second, still more fundamental difference between Bible and Bavli. The Christian canon reached closure with the Bible: Old and New Testaments. The Judaic Torah never closed; revelation of Torah continued.[1] The Torah is not the Bible, and the Bible is not the Torah. The difference in process leading to Bible and Bavli, respectively, has been spelled out in my brief summaries of two distinct histories. The Bible emerges from the larger process of establishing church order and doctrine.[2] The Torah ('Oral and Written') for its part derives from the larger process of working out in relationship to the Pentateuchal system the authority and standing of two successive and connected systems that had followed, the Mishnah and then the Bavli. But the problem solved for Christianity by the Bible and for Judaism by the Bavli is one and the same problem. And that is one not of literature, let alone mere logic of cogent discourse. It is the problem of relating ongoing history to a well-composed culture, change to continuity, the newest generation to the enduring social world and, in the deep reality of the heart and soul, daughters to mothers and sons to fathers.

Let me therefore conclude with a point relevant to this conference in general, which is the observation that thought always proceeds in a context, whether one of logic and process or proposition and proportion and composition. And context always is social. A longstanding problem faced all system-builders in the tradition that commenced

1.   So too did the pattern of Christian truth, but in a different form and forum from the canonical Bible.

2.   I cannot pretend to know whether or not von Campenhausen's arguments about the emergence of the New Testament in response to Montanism prove valid. I can flatly state that the issue—providing a base to sort out the claims of living prophets, with direct access to divine teachings—bears no point of intersection, let alone comparison and contrast, with anything known to me in the entire corpus of rabbinic writing of late antiquity.

with the Pentateuch. From that original system onward system-builders, both in Judaism and, as we now realize, in Christianity, would have to represent their system not as an original statement on its own, but as part of a tradition of revealed truth. Not only this, but in the passage of time and in the accumulation of writing, intellectuals, both Christian and Judaic, would have to work out a logic that would permit cogent discourse with and within the inherited traditions. In the Christian case, the solution to the problem lay in accepting as canonical a variety of documents, each with its own logic. We note, for instance, that extraordinarily cogent communication could be accomplished, in some Christian writings, through symbol and not through proposition at all. Christian writings exhibit their own individual coherent logical principles of cogency, with the making of connections and the drawing of conclusions fully consistent throughout.

The final solution of the canon sidestepped the problem of bringing these logics together within a single statement. If diverse logics work, each for its own authoritative writing, then I really do not have to effect coherence among diverse logics at all, and the canon, the conception of the Bible, would impose from without a cogency of discourse difficult to discern in the interior of the canonical writings. That decision would then dictate the future of the Christian intellectual enterprise: to explore the underbrush of the received writing and to straighten out the tangled roots. No wonder, then, that in philosophy, culminating in the return to Athens, the Christian mind would recover that glory of logical and systematic order denied it in the dictated canon, the Bible. But the canon did solve the problem that faced the heirs to a rather odd corpus of writing. Ignoring logic as of no account, accepting considerable diversity in modes of making connections and drawing conclusions, the traditional solution represented a better answer than the librarians of the Essenes at Qumran had found, which was to set forth (so far as matters now seem at any rate) neither a system nor a canon.

The Bavli's authorship was the first in the history of Judaism, encompassing Christianity in its earliest phases,[1] to take up, on behalf

---

1. I do not mean to ignore the school of Matthew and the numerous other Christian writers who cited prooftexts for their propositions. But as we have seen in the case of the Judaic counterparts, merely citing prooftexts is not the same thing as setting forth a complete system in the form of a tradition, such as was done by the Bavli's authorship.

of its distinct and distinctive system, a position of relationship with the received heritage of tradition, with a corpus of truth assigned to God's revelation to Moses at Sinai. The framers of the Pentateuch did not do so; rather they said that what they wrote was the work of God, dictated to Moses at Sinai. The Essene librarians at Qumran did not do so. They collected this and that, never even pretending that everything fitted together in some one way, not as commentary to Scripture (though some wrote commentaries), not as systemic statements (though the library included such statements), and not as a canon (unless everything we find in the detritus forms a canon by definition). The authorship of the Mishnah did not do so. Quite on the contrary, it undertook the pretense that, even when Scripture supplied facts and dictated the order of those facts, their writing was new and fresh and their own.[1] No wonder that the Mishnah's authorship resorted to its own logic to make its own statement in its own language and for its own purposes. No wonder, too, that the hubris of the Mishnah's authorship provoked the systematic demonstration of the dependence of the Mishnah on Scripture—but also the allegation that the Mishnah stood as an autonomous statement, another Torah, the oral one, equal in value to the Written Torah. The hubris of the great intellects of Judaic and Christian antiquity, the daring authorships of the Pentateuch and the Mishnah, the great ecclesiastical minds behind the Bible, reached its boldest realization in the Bavli. This authorship accomplished, as we have seen, through its ingenious joining of two distinct and contradictory logics of cogent discourse the statement of the Torah in its own rhetoric, following its own logic, and in accord with its own designated topical program. But hubris is not the sole trait that characterizes the Jewish mind, encompassing its Christian successors, in classical times.

1. The best example is the Mishnah tractate *Yoma*, chs. 1–7, which follows the order of Leviticus 16 and reviews its rite, step by step, rarely citing the pertinent chapter of Scripture and never conceding that all that was in hand was a summary and paraphrase of rules available elsewhere. It is a simple fact that we cannot make any sense at all out of that tractate without a point by point consultation with Leviticus 16. But there are numerous other examples of mere paraphrasing, by Mishnah's authorship, of passages of Scripture (along with many more where Scripture has nothing to say on topics dealt with in the Mishnah, or in which what Scripture thinks important about a topic is simply ignored as of no interest in the Mishnah).

There is a second trait common to them all. It is that in all systemic constructions and statements[1] the issues of logic responded to the systemic imperative and in no way dictated the shape and structure of that imperative. The system invariably proves to be prior, recapitulating itself, also, in its logic. And however diverse the issues addressed by various systems made up by the Jewish mind in classical times, all had to address a single question natural to the religious ecology in which Judaic systems flourished. That question, in the aftermath of the Pentateuchal system, concerned how people could put together in a fresh construction and a composition of distinctive proportions a statement that purported to speak truth to a social entity that, in the nature of things, already had truth. This framing of the issue of how system contradicts tradition, how the logic that tells me to make a connection of this to that, but not to the other thing, and to draw from that connection one conclusion, rather than some other— that framing of the issue places intellect, the formation of mind and modes of thought squarely into the ongoing processes dictated by the givens of society.

Why then characterize the Bavli's system-builders as the climax of the hubris of the Jewish intellectuals? Because the Bavli's authorship was the first in the history of Judaism, encompassing Christianity in its earliest phases, to take up, in behalf of its distinct and distinctive system, a considered position of relationship with the received heritage of tradition, with a corpus of truth assigned to God's revelation to Moses at Sinai. Four centuries after the Mishnah, in their mind eighteen centuries after God revealed the Torah to Moses at Mount Sinai, the Bavli's authorship remade the two received systems, the Pentateuchal and the mishnaic. In its own rhetoric, in accord with its own topical programme, appealing to a logic unique to itself among all Jewish minds in ancient times, that authorship presented the Torah of Sinai precisely as it wished to present it. And it did so defiantly, not discreetly and by indirection. Not merely alleging that Moses had written it all down, like the Pentateuchal compilers, nor modestly identifying with the direction of the Holy Spirit the choices that it made, like the Christians responsible for making the Bible, nor even, as with the framers of the Mishnah, sedulously sidestepping, in laconic and disingenuous innocence, the issue of authority and

---

1. The two are not the same.

tradition entirely. Quite the opposite; the Bavli's intellectuals took over the entire tradition, scriptural and mishnaic alike, chose what they wanted, tacked on to the selected passages their own words in their own way, and then put it all out as a single statement of their own.

True, they claimed for their system the standing of a mere amplification of that tradition. But, as a matter of fact, they did say it all in their own words and they did set forth the whole of their statement in their own way. Above all, without recapitulating the traditional choices of ignoring or merely absorbing the received revelation, they represented what they themselves had made up as the one whole Torah revealed by God to Moses, our rabbi, at Sinai, and they made it stick. And that, I think, is the supreme hubris of the Jewish mind from the beginnings, in the Pentateuch, to the conclusion and climax in the Bavli. I like to think that that hubris of theirs explains the success of what they made up,[1] on the simple principle that the more daring, the more plausible. For theirs was the final realization and statement in the formation of the Jewish intellect. And that is a considerable fact, worthy of the attention of anyone interested in the power of sacred writings to shape society: the sociology of sacred texts.

---

1. But of course the reason for the Bavli's enormous authority throughout the world of Judaism from Islamic times to ours cannot in the end be merely aesthetic.

Index of Names